ld in 159 Days

Acclaim for *Dare to Dream*

Doug's story is one of limitless possibilities. He proves that anything is possible—regardless of the circumstance or challenge you face. You must dare to dream or get out of the dreamer's way. Diabetes, as Doug illustrates, can be the challenge that makes you great.

> —Nicole Johnson Baker
> Miss America 1999

Dare to Dream: Flying Solo with Diabetes is a truly inspirational story of one man's life and his tremendous struggle to conquer many barriers and obstacles to reach his skyward dreams. Douglas Cairns did more than fly solo around the world in a small plane to fulfill his dream of being a pilot after losing his license; he also sent a strong, clear message that all people should follow their dreams and let nothing get in the way…not even diabetes.

While reading *Dare to Dream,* I found myself daydreaming about being in the cockpit flying around the globe, meeting my blood brothers with diabetes living and struggling with this condition. I could feel how it would be to test, inject, eat and fight fatigue at several thousand feet above the earth for hours and hours at a time…alone. I was inspired by Douglas' motivation, drive, bravery and desire to uplift the spirit of anyone put down and grounded by diabetes. Douglas may have flown solo with diabetes, but his accomplishments were for all of us down here on earth with life's challenges.

> —Steven Edelman MD
> Taking Control of Your Diabetes

Life is about choices. We have basically two choices. Either we *can* do something or we *can't*. Your glass can be *half full* or *half empty*. This is a story of someone who has made a conscious decision that his glass will be at least half full. It is an inspiration to read how it is possible with determination and discipline to overcome any problem that life throws at you. What is even more inspiring is to see how Douglas has not only controlled his own destiny, but through patient example, he has questioned authority and bureaucratic decisions in such a way as to be truly effective and influential in mobilizing change.

This story has two definite dimensions, and it is impossible to classify one as being greater than the other. Here is a man who has conquered huge disappointment and gone forward as an example to the world. He shows in this book how he has disciplined himself to control his life. On top of this he has taken on and succeeded at one of the world's most extreme challenges. Flying around the world is no mean feat for those without a challenging medical condition, and Douglas has displayed a limitless raft of courage and bravery throughout a gruelling and demanding journey. On top of all this, he won the hearts and minds of everyone he encountered. He has gained the love and respect of us all.

> —Polly Vacher, MBE
> Wings Around the World in aid of Flying Scholarships for the Disabled

I was pleased to read Douglas Cairns' inspiring description of his experiences flying around the world in spite of having diabetes. He is pushing the boundaries for someone with diabetes. In the long run, this will help to decrease discrimination. Doug and his book are an inspiration for all of us.

> —H. Peter Chase, M.D.
> Barbara Davis Center for Childhood Diabetes

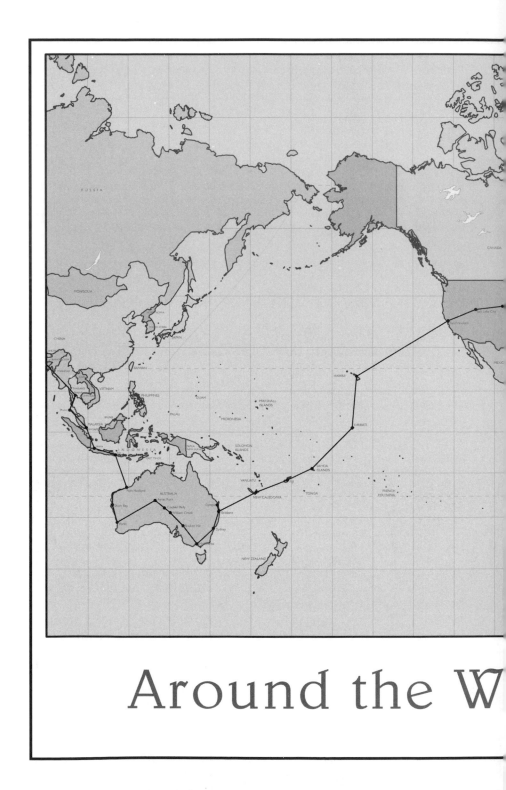

Around the W

Douglas Cairns

Dare
to
Dream
FLYING SOLO WITH DIABETES

*Around the world
in 159 days*

Albyne Press

A catalogue record for this book is available from the British Library.

ISBN 0-9549929-0-3

Library of Congress Control Number: 2005902275

Albyne Press Limited, Invergloy House, Spean Bridge, Inverness-shire, PH34 4DY.
Albyne Press, 1221 Pearl Street, Boulder, CO, 80302.

Editor, Sherrye Landrum; *Composition,* Jim Stein;
Cover Design, Rikki Campbell Ogden; *Printer,* Cadmus, Port City Press Division.

For special promotion or bulk orders, please contact the publisher.
Visit our website at www.albynepress.com

Lower back cover photo: Northern coastline of "La Grande Terre," New Caledonia

Printed in the U.S.A.

Contents

Foreword

You're holding in your hands one of the most remarkable adventure stories ever written—and one of the most inspirational!

Until recently, people with type 1 diabetes (formerly called *juvenile diabetes*) were limited in what they could do. Children with diabetes were discouraged from participating in gym class, much less competitive sports. As adults, their vocational choices were limited. Whole categories of employment—soldier, truck driver, fireman, policeman, pilot—were strictly off limits.

In recent years, the tools available to control diabetes have improved *dramatically*. With better monitors for testing blood sugar levels and greatly improved, more predictable insulins, the danger of low blood sugar episodes has been significantly reduced. Doors that once were closed to people with diabetes are slowly being opened. Bold pioneers are *charging* through those doors to do things that were unimaginable just ten years ago.

Douglas Cairns is at the very top of the list of these modern-day heroes who defy the challenges of their disease—and their own fears—to prove that people with diabetes can do *anything*, as long as they keep their blood sugars under tight control. His story is a shining example to people with diabetes, and it is equally powerful and motivational to anyone who faces challenges or obstacles of any kind.

Doctors originally told Douglas that diabetes made his childhood dream to fly impossible. But his story proves that a dream is a hard thing to kill. If we have the courage, and the persistence, sometimes it is within our power to do what others say cannot be done.

Lance Porter
Author of *28 Days to Diabetes Control!*

Introduction

When once you have tasted flight, you will forever walk the earth with your eyes turned skyward, for there you have been, and there you will always long to return.

—Leonardo da Vinci

In 1989 at the age of 25, I was a Royal Air Force jet instructor in the U.K., carrying out my boyhood dream to fly. I loved my work; I loved flying. And then, I began to lose weight and to feel tired. After I had lost 26 pounds and had felt continually fatigued for six weeks straight, a military doctor did a blood test and delivered a blunt message, "You are a diabetic, and you *were* a pilot."

In one sentence, my dreams were blown away. My pancreas had stopped producing insulin. I required injections of insulin every day to stay alive. A disciplined diet, blood sugar testing, plenty of exercise, and visits to the doctor were all now required for me to be in good health. The risk of low blood sugars—hypoglycemia—and passing out were the reasons I would no longer be permitted to pilot an aircraft anywhere in the world.

On February 19, 2003, fourteen years after being diagnosed, I sat alone in a Beech Baron B58 twin-engine aircraft, pulled the engine throttles back, lifted the nose and waited for the aircraft to settle onto the runway below. It was a crisp, sunny, winter day in Iowa, U.S. At the moment I touched earth, I had completed 63 flights over 26,300 nautical miles, passing through 22 countries. Five months earlier I had taken off from this same airport, headed east. I had completed Diabetes World Flight, a dream to fly around the world at the controls of an aircraft as a licensed pilot.

My aims were clear: 1) To show aviation authorities around the world—in a positive and constructive way—that flying with type 1 diabetes is safe according to the U.S. Federal Aviation Administration (FAA) system. 2) To show everyone that diabetes need not limit the scope of a person's dreams and ambitions.

Diabetes World Flight was an amazing personal flying experience, and an eye-opening journey through our "global diabetes epidemic." As I flew around the world, I learned how diabetes is putting severe pressure on health-care systems in many countries, and how difficult life can be for individuals with diabetes who live in developing countries. I heard about people with diabetes suffering appalling discrimination in society and in the workplace, so that they kept their disease hidden and did not take care of it. In some countries, medicine was too expensive to afford. In others, insulin was not even available. In one country, where the average annual wage was $4,000, diabetes patients with kidney complications had only two options: "Find $50,000 or die."

There were lighthearted moments, too. Besides making new friends and getting to visit old friends, I delighted in watching dolphins and whales swimming in the oceans beneath the plane and met a lovable diabetic dog in Australia, an active member of his local diabetes support group—a group that has kept a sense of humor. In every country, I saw proof that the global diabetes community is vibrant and strong. It is a powerful force for people and families living with diabetes.

Dare to Dream: Flying Solo with Diabetes is the story of my life with diabetes, shattered dreams, a new career, and a wonderful return to flying and the realization of a dream to fly around the world as a licensed pilot. The past three years have been the most enlightening and fulfilling of my life. It is a real pleasure to share the highlights with you now. Enjoy the journey....

Chapter:

1 Boyhood Dreams

The desire to fly is an idea handed down to us by our ancestors who, in their grueling travels across trackless lands in prehistoric times, looked enviously on the birds soaring freely through space, at full speed, above all obstacles, on the infinite highway of the air.
—Wilbur Wright

A Passion for Speed

I grew up in Lochaber in the Scottish Highlands, a popular flight training area for the Royal Air Force (RAF). As a young lad, I remember military jets roaring overhead at 250 feet. I was captivated as Jaguar and Phantom fighters flew along the Great Glen and wheeled around 3,000-foot mountains as if they were molehills. My Dad tells me that when I was eight years old, I ran into the house one day after watching a jet scream overhead and exclaimed, "I'm going to fly those one day!"

At the age of eight, I flew for the first time on a domestic flight from Scotland to London. I was enthralled. Takeoff was exhilarating, and once aloft, I savored the bird's eye view of the countryside and clouds below. I was hooked on flying from my first airborne moment.

As I grew older, I developed a passion for speed. Speed in cars, bicycles, and on skis. Undoubtedly, the speed, noise and raw power of low-flying jets appealed enormously to me.

Soon after my 18th birthday, I took a flying lesson in a tiny Cessna 152 at Inverness Airport. It was bliss, climbing into the air sitting alongside a 70-year-old ex-World War II Spitfire pilot. Halfway through the flight, we spotted a RAF Jaguar fast jet passing below us at five times our speed. The instructor already knew that flying fighters was my ambition. He leaned over and shouted above the engine noise, "You'll be flying one of those in a few years!" I wished so hard it hurt.

As a lad, I played lots of sports—rugby, tennis and golf—and hiked the hills near home, always running back down the slopes at full pelt. Skiing became a passion. My father had been one of Scotland's ski pioneers, trudging up 4,000-foot mountains for hours and speeding back down in minutes. (Not even a rope tow to help him get up the slope again!) Skiing was in the blood. I also loved the crisp mountain air, stunning views of the valleys below, and the exhilarating speed I could reach on two planks of wood.

At the age of 12, I was introduced to slalom and giant slalom ski racing, competing in the British and Scottish Junior Championships. Racing against the clock and other skiers was addictive. I soon lived and breathed skiing, training continually and much to my delight, joining the British "Citadin" Team (effectively the British "B" Team) at the age of 16. I was fit, undertaking intense training sessions six times a week. I was keen to take some "time out" from school to pursue a racing career.

Then at 16, I fractured and chipped my third and fourth vertebrae during a downhill ski race in France. Fortunately the damage did not threaten the spinal chord, but a condition called osteocondritis set in, which prevented the damaged bone from healing. The only way to cure it was to stop all bone-jarring sports. My ski-racing ambitions were suddenly over. It was a bitter blow. I decided to return to my plans for a University degree and becoming a pilot.

The Royal Air Force

The requirements for military jet flying are demanding. I needed minimum academic qualifications, preferably higher-level mathematics and physics—even better, a degree. I had to be medically "A1" with perfect eyesight. Good hand-to-eye coordination was required, along with strong teamwork and leadership skills.

I had concerns about my abilities and suitability. While I knew I was athletic and this should help, I wasn't mechanically minded. After passing "O levels" (at age 16), I found higher mathematics a nightmare. I was also worried that I would not meet the leadership qualities required of an officer in the RAF. However, I was okay at mental arithmetic; I could calculate sums in my head, which is something that pilots need to be able to do. I was also passionate about flying fast jets.

I first applied at 17 for a University Cadetship (sponsorship) for studying Geography at Edinburgh University. I wasn't selected. The letter from the RAF outlined that I did, however, have some of the qualities they were looking for, and that I should try again in two year's time. I decided to try to improve identified weaknesses—mathematics and leadership qualities—for the next application.

In my first year at the University, I applied to join the University Air Squadron (UAS) as a Volunteer Reserve (part-time member). The UAS was a known recruiting medium for future pilots, an excellent "back door" entry into the RAF. Selected students learned to fly, receiving about 30 hours of tuition a year. At Edinburgh Airport, there were four full-time RAF flying instructors teaching students on small-piston, single-engine, two seater, British Aerospace Bulldog aircraft. These were sporty little machines capable of 120 knots cruise at low level, and they were fully aerobatic. If I could get in and show aptitude for flying, it would help my next application to the RAF.

The UAS interviews progressed well, but I failed the medical due to my back condition. An X-ray showed that the chipped area around the fourth vertebrae had not yet filled in, and I still suffered some discomfort around the lumbar region. I applied again in my second year and much to my relief, the chipped bone had begun to heal. It was enough to pass the medical. That was it! I could now become a member of the UAS and learn to fly at the University.

Joining the UAS gave me a new lease on life. I took flying lessons at least once a week, with a like-minded, fun-loving bunch of guys. In the meantime, I thoroughly enjoyed my University studies, my back condition had improved, and I had returned to competitive skiing with the University Ski Team. I was also going out with Kirsty, a lovely girl from Stranraer in southwest Scotland. Life couldn't have been better.

In the first year, I flew 60 hours and applied for a RAF cadetship again in late 1983. Shortly before Christmas, I attended three days of medical exams, pilot aptitude and general IQ tests, extensive interviews with RAF officers, and then exhaustive teamwork and leadership exercises. I felt that I had done better this time, but would it be enough? I had been enjoying my University courses and had taken on extra-curricular activities and responsibilities with the Ski Team and Ski Club. These would hopefully count in the selection process.

I had a pensive few weeks waiting for the outcome, but in February 1984, I was notified that I had been selected. It was one of life's major moments. As of April 2, 1984, I was Acting Pilot Officer D. R. Cairns RAF. My dreams and ambitions were coming true.

First Solo

In my two and a half years in the UAS, I completed 160 hours of flying, learning general handling skills, basic instrument flying (in cloud), navigation and aerobatics. I particularly enjoyed aerobatics—loops, stall turns, barrel rolls, slow rolls, four-point rolls, Cuban eights and more. There's nothing quite like flying upside down!

I had been apprehensive about some of the theory, particularly the mechanical and mathematical parts. While it required hard work, it seemed to be more straightforward than I originally expected, thanks to a progressive and logical learning process. Some of the subjects, including aerodynamics and meteorology, I found fascinating.

The first time flying solo is a major milestone for any pilot. After I had about 10 hours of training with numerous practice landings and takeoffs, the instructor climbed out and said, "Now go and do the same on your own." Without the instructor, the little Bulldog was lighter and accelerated noticeably faster down the runway. While apprehensive, I was elated. I was on my own, totally responsible for my actions, nobody to intervene should things go wrong.

First solo in any RAF aircraft attracts some celebration. At East Lowlands' UAS, the celebration took the form of drinking "The Horn"—two feet of hollow animal horn containing three and a half pints of beer. One guy stood on the bar and then walked up and down its full length while drinking this

3.5-pint monster. At the end of the bar, he slowly lowered the Horn, belched loudly, stuck his head out of an open window and vomited. What a performance! My own was much less impressive.

Officer Training

I graduated from Edinburgh University in 1985, having enjoyed my studies, learned to fly and recaptured my love of ski racing. In my final year, I took four weeks off my winter term to join the RAF Ski Team, competing against the British Army and Navy Teams. It had been a fulfilling four years and much lay ahead.

At the end of summer 1985, I attended the Initial Officer Training Course (IOT) at RAF College Cranwell, a historic World War II base in Lincolnshire, England. For 18 weeks, the 120 trainees were split into teams of 10 cadets with a Flight Lieutenant in charge of training us. After the freedom of student life, the rigid military training was a terrible shock to the system. One's status was suddenly "zero" (more like −10). From organizing your own study time and having total freedom during long holidays, life now devolved into early wake-up calls, room inspections, parades, drill sessions with feisty flight sergeants, rigorous physical training and leadership exercises. At times it was misery. At other times, there was a great feeling of achievement and camaraderie.

I was elated to be withdrawn for two of the last four weeks of IOT to join the RAF Ski Team in the European Alps. I was physically fit on joining the team, but having missed three weeks of race training, I was slower than the previous year. However, I was back in the Italian Alps with crisp clear air, stunning mountainous scenery and the joys of skiing. I couldn't think of a better way to spend two weeks of IOT.

When I returned to RAF Cranwell, there were only two weeks of IOT remaining, and I'd missed graduation parade preparations. On my first parade drill, after I muddled into the back row, Warrant Officer Pike roared, "FORWAAARD, MARCH!" I stumbled out of step, feeling like a fool. WO Pike roared again, "CAIRNS! WHERE HAVE YOU BEEEEN? ON HOL-IDAY?" I shouted back, with little disguised satisfaction, "YES, SIR!" I had to wait behind and explain myself to one very exasperated Warrant Officer.

Immediately after the IOT graduation ceremony, one of my course-mates, Rich Watson, and I drove over to the junior officer cadets' barracks to receive a few snappy salutes from junior officer cadets. In retrospect this was very poor form, but we just couldn't resist the temptation.

Basic Jet Flying Training

I will never forget the first day of ground school when our Chief Ground School Instructor told us that out of our group of 12 we could expect two to be dead before the end of our careers. Tragically, as of the time of this writing, his prediction is accurate. Two of our original colleagues have died in air crashes.

Jet training began after IOT, with three months of solid ground school on the Jet Provost TMk V (JP5). Once the flying started, we were under immense pressure. We all knew that if we failed two consecutive trips, we would most likely be chopped from training.

Twelve of us completed the 63 Basic Flying Training School (BFTS) Course over 15 months. There was a collegiate atmosphere with constant banter (quite fierce at times). After ground school finished, we flew in the Jet Provost TMk5 (JP5), a 30-year-old, two-seater machine capable of 450 mph—a powerful sports car compared to the Bulldog and a solid stepping stone to fast jets. The JP5 was a big change. Its jet engine whined smoothly behind the side-by-side seats, while a Bulldog's piston engine vibrated away loudly in front. The JP was much larger and faster. We consolidated our existing skills and learned new ones—close formation flying (just feet away from other aircraft), instrument flying in cloud, night flying and low-level navigation. Flying 250 feet above the ground at 300 knots was exhilarating. There is a rush of speed while you focus 100% on the job at hand—trying to navigate accurately and safely.

At the end of the 15-month course, there was a low-level navigation and aerobatics contest. I was honored to compete against Keith Collister (one of my two course-mates who have died) in a navigation competition, being judged by the Chief Flying Instructor, Wing Commander Mike Cross.

Little did I know that I would meet Mike Cross 15 years later as part of Diabetes World Flight. Astonishingly, he had type 1 diabetes when we flew together. He had recognized his diabetes symptoms after his son had been diagnosed some years earlier, but was desperate not to lose his flying career, determined not to allow it to affect his life. He had found a way to manage his diabetes in private. Keeping it undetected from the military until retirement at 55 years of age was quite a feat. So good was his control that it went undetected despite detailed annual physicals for 18 years; a testament to diligent and disciplined control.

It is amusing to recall this navigation competition flight. It started at medium level from Lincolnshire followed by low level at 250 feet for a simulated bombing run in Wales. Half an hour into the flight, Wing Commander Cross instructed me to divert to RAF Shawbury to the northeast. I had a fair idea of where we were, but after fumbling around with the maps, I was soon lost. I eventually blustered my way into the circuit pattern at Shawbury, bitterly disappointed. Not surprisingly, Keith won the competition by quite a margin.

Fast Jet Flying Training

Shortly after finishing at Cranwell, we began Advanced Flying Training at RAF Valley on the Isle of Anglesey. This island, perched on the northwest tip of Wales, is a desolate, wind-swept, and at times, miserable place. However, I couldn't have been happier. The Hawk was a sleek single-engine fast jet trainer capable of 550 knots straight-line speed and supersonic in a dive. I was literally on cloud nine every time I climbed in.

The new aircraft was considerably faster than the JP5, and it took time to get used to this. The JP5 climbed at 140 knots and about 2,000 feet per minute. In the Hawk, you accelerated to 300 knots in a shallow climb before raising the nose 10 degrees and "nailing" 6,000 feet per minute climb rate. Low-level cruise speed increased from 300 knots to 420 knots, 7 nautical miles a minute. We had to wear G-suits to counteract up to 5 Gs in maximum-rate turns and aerobatics. Every flight required extensive preparations. I sat for hours in a simulator cockpit, memorizing lengthy cockpit and emergency drill checklists. Despite the exhilaration of flying such a powerful and sleek machine, there was no time to sit back and appreciate the ride. We had to be totally focused, always trying to be thinking "ahead of the aircraft."

After 30 hours, we sat a basic handling test. Halfway through, the hydraulics-system warning lit up, and the test had to be cut short. The examiner took control, and we returned to home base. The test was, therefore, split over two flights, and in between, my nerves got the better of me. On the second flight, I flew badly, mishandled a simulated emergency and failed.

I was terribly disappointed, and extremely worried about passing the re-sit. The following two days were nerve-racking, as I was memorizing and practicing emergency procedures over and over again. The knowledge that we were only two trips away from being chopped weighed heavily. It was an *enormous* relief to pass on the second attempt.

Some memorable flights stand out: Low level at 420 knots around Wales's coastline, cruising inland and then pulling up sharply with 4 Gs to punch through holes in clouds above. Battle formation (where a Hawk flew 100 m behind another, offset at a 30-degree angle) through the Lake District mountains, pulling up fast over a valley head and rolling upside down to pull back down into the next valley. *That* was immense fun. Flying low-level around the waters of the Scottish Hebrides, again in battle formation. The western Scottish Isles possess mystical beauty, and at one point, I looked around over calm waters and caught a glimpse of a yacht mast flashing by at eye-level. Tremendous stuff!

Another outstanding experience was flying over my home near Fort William in the Scottish Highlands. Years before, I had watched a Hawker Hunter fast-jet pass in front of the house, pull up sharply and turn steeply over the summit of the 1,800-foot mountain behind the house. *What utter freedom!* I did exactly the same maneuver in the Hawk, pulling 4 Gs up over the house, soaring over the mountaintop in a steep turn and descending sharply in the opposite direction into Glen Gloy, a remote and barren valley that I'd cycled and jogged through countless times as a lad.

Most pilots have stories to tell, and during training, I had a couple of "close shaves." During a formation flight (of three Hawk aircraft flying close together) over North Wales, course-mate Keith, flying on the inside of a right-hand turn, shouted sharply over the radio. He had seen another formation flight pass incredibly close to ours, but being on the outside of a turn (focusing only on the lead aircraft), I had been blissfully unaware. On the ground, Keith told us just how close we had come to disaster. It was food for thought.

In the previous year, I had been flying a low-level exercise around the Highlands of Scotland with my instructor. We planned to fly over my old school and then home, so I rang my parents to let them know when we would pass by. Home is a stunningly beautiful spot, sitting prominently above the shores of Loch Lochy, a small oasis of landscaped trees and gardens laid down

100 years earlier. As we wheeled over the house in a tight turn, my parents rushed out onto the lawn and waved oilskin coats madly above their heads. Even our Golden Labrador, Russ, was jumping around with all the fun.

The Great Glen runs in a straight line for 100 miles northeast from the western isles to Inverness. All we now had to do was fly 50 miles up the valley to RAF Lossiemouth, just beyond Inverness. However, a few miles up the valley sat a very obvious snowstorm. I suggested diverting back to Spean Bridge, just five miles away and heading up a clear valley to Aviemore. However, the instructor told me to press on and "have a look" through the snowstorm.

It was certainly quite a look. Two minutes later, cloud brushed over the canopy and snow began to fall heavily, reducing visibility to dangerously low levels. The instructor took over. A chink of brighter light lay off to the east in a higher valley, so he banked and climbed higher, cautiously nosing into this brighter area. It was a big mistake. Our speed had slowed from 300 knots to 150 knots. We were wallowing around with low energy, not much use if you need to pull up and climb away quickly from the ground.

Almost immediately we entered cloud, and with mountains close by, the instructor initiated an "emergency low-level abort," applying full power and climbing as steeply as possible. I looked at the map. We were at 1,000 feet while the mist-shrouded mountains close by were 3,000 feet high. *Bloody Hell!* As we clawed our way higher, I had black thoughts about what it would feel like to hit one of those mountains. The cockpit would cave in, crushing us instantly. At least it would be quick. I thought of my parents. I was incredibly ANGRY with the instructor, thinking somewhat ironically to myself, *If we crash, I'll KILL you!* We could have safely diverted back by Spean Bridge.

It was a classic accident scenario. The crash report could have read something like this: *The Jet Provost was seen circling over the student pilot's parents' home at 1520 Hours. The aircraft then proceeded northeast along the Great Glen into a snowstorm. At 1523 a farmer near Fort Augustus heard a lone jet pass overhead in heavy snowfall, followed by the sound of a major impact.* It would have been terrible for my family.

As we climbed through 3,000 feet, I felt enormous relief. However, clear ice was streaming back from the leading edges of the wings; we weren't out of trouble yet. Moments later we burst into clear air. Thirty miles ahead, snow-covered Cairngorm Mountains basked in brilliant afternoon sunlight, a beautiful and welcome sight. We sat silently for a few moments, the engine whining reassuringly, and then my instructor said "Hmm. These low level aborts are quite thought-provoking, aren't they?" Yes, they are.

The Hawk fast-jet training finished with a "Final Handling Test" with close formation and battle formation flying; low-level navigation with "time over target;" general handling with stalls, spins, steep turns and aerobatics and simulated emergency handling. On the simulated bombing run, I diverted round a heavy rain shower and was surprised (and delighted) to flash over the tiny target telephone box, just on time. The final few minutes comprised a simulated engine failure, with a radar-PFL (glide descent through cloud followed by practice forced landing) straight back into RAF Valley. The memory of my earlier failed test haunted me. However, I squeaked this simulated emergency landing in ok. No frills, but safely. Whew!

I passed the test. After two and a half years of training (and $4 million of taxpayers' money), I had finally earned my "fast-jet wings." It had been extremely hard work with intense pressure all the way through—and it had been worth every single bit of effort. I was living my boyhood dream.

Instructor Pilot

At the end of Advanced Flying Training, I was selected for instructor training on Jet Provosts. This meant a five-month course followed by two and a half years of instructing before progressing on to front-line jets and operational flying. Part of me was frustrated to have front-line flying delayed by three years, the other felt honored to be selected.

Overall the RAF was my perfect career. I loved the freedom of being airborne, the thrill of flying fast in sophisticated aircraft. I skied with the RAF Ski Team every season for up to five weeks in the European Alps and competed with the British Combined Services Ski Team in Australia each year. What a combination for me—flying *and* skiing!

When I was a teenager, ski racing was comprised of early wake-up calls, long runs, intense ski training, followed by further fitness (more like exhaustion) training, waxing skis and early nights. The RAF skiing was serious training and racing, yet serious fun with a highly spirited and likeable bunch of lads—with a few beers thrown in. My individual ski racing became part of the team effort. I loved it.

In my first year of RAF racing, I joined the British Combined Services Ski Team, and seven of us traveled to Australia to compete against the local military ski teams. I had never been to Australia before, and while traveling there, we passed through Manila, the capital of the Philippines, a brief but fascinating visit. Training and racing was held in Thredbo, Australia's premiere ski resort. The laid-back Australian approach to life, punctuated heavily with a raw, dry sense of humor, appealed greatly. That first trip to the Australian Alps was quite a life changer. I met and fell in love with a slim, vivacious, fun-loving girl named Chrissy. Three years later we were married.

The year of 1988 was a busy one. I gained my Qualified Flying Instructor rating over a five-month course in Lincolnshire. I skied with the RAF Ski Team in January and February and again with the British Services Ski Team in Australia in August. Immediately afterward, we were married in Orange— not the color, but Chrissy's hometown in New South Wales, Australia.

In September 1988, a month after our wedding, we set up home together in York, just 14 miles from RAF Linton-on-Ouse where I was posted to instruct. It was an ideal situation. It was exciting to start married life, and particularly good that Chrissy was able to continue her promising career in public relations consulting after finding a job in York. Meanwhile flying instructing was hard work but rewarding over the following months. I felt inexperienced to instruct with only 440 hours in my logbook and no operational flying. (Compared to many new civilian instructors, this is pretty good experience.) It was fulfilling to teach, watching students gain new skills. At times the pace was intense with up to four trips a day. Each flight lasted an hour, requiring focused concentration from both student and instructor. I remember feeling fatigued at times. However, this was strange for me. It was possible that diabetes was beginning to bubble away—reduced insulin means reduced energy. Little did I know what was about to happen.

Chapter:

2 Shattered Dreams

Science, freedom, beauty, adventure: what more could you ask of life? Aviation combined all the elements I loved.
— Charles A. Lindbergh

The major difference between a thing that might go wrong and a thing that cannot possibly go wrong is that when a thing that cannot possibly go wrong goes wrong it usually turns out to be impossible to get at or repair.
— Douglas Adams

Something Was Wrong

Just before Christmas 1988, I came down with the flu and took more than 10 days to recover. Afterward, I didn't feel quite right. I felt tired, and over a period of six weeks, I gradually developed a raging thirst and had to urinate frequently. I was losing weight.

I also behaved like a classic pilot. Although I suspected something was wrong, I didn't want to go to the doctor for fear of losing my flying medical. I didn't feel physically unwell, just fatigued and passing lots of water. I convinced myself it could be a "post-viral fatigue syndrome" from the earlier flu.

When I left my parents' home after Christmas, I kissed my sister, a doctor, goodbye, and she quietly said, "Go to the doctor when you get back to the base.

You have a sweet smell on your breath, which could be a sign of high blood sugar." She had detected ketones, a distinct sweet/bitter smell that can be present when one is losing weight rapidly, and is also associated with diabetes. I visited the base doctor the next day for a blood test but for whatever reason, no result came back. It would be another six weeks before I was diagnosed.

A week later, I flew a low-level cross-country training flight with a student to RAF Leuchars in Fife, north of Edinburgh. While crossing the Firth of Forth and approaching Fife, the distant coastline looked blurred. That was odd—normally my eyesight was 20/20. I had no idea that this was high blood sugar changing the viscosity of my eyeball fluids. (This reverses soon after blood sugars are normalized.) I also remember being ravenously hungry. In the squadron crew room, I ate copious amounts of toast, dripping with honey. I was steadily losing weight. There was insufficient insulin to convert the food I ate into energy. The only way for my body to gain energy was to break down fat reserves and muscle.

In mid-January, I joined the RAF Ski Squad in Tignes, a resort at 6,000 feet in the French Alps, where the RAF Championships were being held. It was a nightmare. I was tired, weak, and had a raging thirst. I now needed to pass water frequently, making lots of yellow snow. With low humidity in the Alps, I was incredibly thirsty. My strength seemed noticeably sapped, and I couldn't race as quickly as the year before. Each slalom course inspection required stepping up its entire length. I could only take a few steps at a time before having to stop to recover from exhaustion. One evening I felt nauseated for no apparent reason and slept, fitfully, for almost 12 hours, waking up every couple of hours to urinate. By the second week in February, six weeks after recovering from the flu, I had lost 26 pounds. For someone whose normal weight was only 154 pounds, I was painfully thin. A couple of the ski team members commented on it. That was enough; I decided to go to the Station doctor as soon as I returned to base.

When I returned to York, Chrissy was shocked to see me looking so skinny, and she burst into tears. She was seriously worried. The next morning I went straight to the medical center and explained how I felt. The symptoms were acute and obvious. A urine sugar test soon showed the culprit.

Diabetes! Bloody Hell! I was told to take the rest of the day off, to avoid eating or drinking large amounts of sweet food or beverages, and to take myself by train the following morning to RAF Ely Hospital near Cambridge. This is where my diabetes would be confirmed and then stabilized.

Reactions

I was devastated. My boyhood dreams had just been shattered. I wouldn't be able to fly anymore. I wondered how I could have diabetes. I had always been fit and healthy, an active sportsman. We had no family history of diabetes. At that moment in time, all I knew about diabetes was what I had heard: people had to inject themselves for the rest of their lives, were generally unhealthy and could die from it. I rang Chrissy and told her the news. It was an emotional few moments. We had only been married for five months, and suddenly everything had changed. We had planned to stay with the RAF until I was 38 years old, another 13 years. This wouldn't be likely now.

I was desperate to find out more about diabetes, and went to the York Public Library to look up a reference book. What I read frightened and depressed me. A book listed the symptoms of diabetes, many of which I had. It then went straight on to list all the long-term diabetes complications including kidney failure (leading to dialysis), neuropathy, leg amputations, blindness and heart disease. It seemed as if these complications were inevitable.

The following day, a doctor at RAF Ely Hospital took a blood test and said, "It's confirmed. You are a diabetic, and you *were* a pilot." (I sincerely hope that this doctor has improved his bedside manner since 1989.) My boyhood dreams to fly were, indeed, shattered.

I was hooked up to an intravenous saline and insulin solution and given two books to read on living with type 1 diabetes. I devoured those two books. I wanted to learn as much as I could about this disease. These books outlined how diabetes could be controlled with a disciplined and sensible approach. If diabetes is well controlled, the long-term health complications could be minimized, and, in fact, avoided. While still devastated and depressed, I was encouraged by this positive advice. I decided on the spot: I wanted to control my diabetes.

Stabilization

Stabilization of my diabetes took 10 days at RAF Ely Hospital. The IV drip gradually re-hydrated me and brought my blood sugars under control. My sugars were tested regularly, and I was awakened each night to ensure that I would not go low. This was all new to me. The nurse would take a finger, prick it with a sharp lancet, put a large blob of blood onto a strip, wipe it clean after one minute and insert the strip into a blood glucose meter. A minute later, a test result appeared. It was an unpleasant process.

I remember how cumbersome the IV drip was, having to wheel it to the restroom with me every few hours. It was a silent, sinister reminder of my condition. One night I rolled over in my sleep and ripped the catheter out of its socket. I woke up with a sharp pain and found IV solution splattering onto the floor. Seeing my horrified reaction, a nurse came over and reconnected the IV.

In two days, my blood sugars dropped toward normal levels, at which time I was taught how to inject. I was not looking forward to this; I had always loathed injections. However, these needles were the same as those used for injecting babies—small. A nurse brought an orange to the table and demonstrated. I pinched some abdomen fat (not much left after losing 26 pounds), took a deep breath and pushed the needle in sharply. While I could feel it go in, the needle didn't hurt.

Many times I couldn't feel the needle going in. Sometimes it felt uncomfortable, on other occasions it stung sharply like an insect bite. (Nowadays I "throw" the needle in. If you push the needle in slowly, there can be more discomfort/pain). I was told to rotate or change the injection sites because lumps could build up under the skin over time. If you inject into these lumps, insulin is not absorbed so well. I could pinch fatty skin on stomach, legs, forearms, and buttocks, but normally I used my stomach. I learned where it was painful to inject and avoided these areas. Even though I'm used to injecting after 16 years, I can still catch myself holding my breath briefly as the needle goes in. I still have an innate dislike of injections.

I wish I could remember the titles of the two books I read at Ely Hospital. They were extremely informative and easy to understand. They stressed the importance of good control and how it can allow people with diabetes to lead a normal life. They fostered my positive attitude toward managing diabetes.

There was much to learn. I had to balance insulin with the carbohydrates I ate, trying to keep sugars within a normal range 72–126 mg/dl (4.0–7.0 mmol/l). However, if I didn't eat enough carbs or took too much insulin, my sugar could go too low or hypoglycemic (hypo). (In the U.K., we call lows *hypos*.) Then, I could develop sweatiness, nausea, headache, shaky hands, tingling lips, irritability, and if it dropped even lower, my condition could deteriorate into impaired thinking, slurred speech and even passing out. If a person passed out for many hours, brain damage and even death could occur.

I learned that severe hypo symptoms can look similar to being drunk. Alcohol on its own lowers blood sugar, so if one was drunk and passed out, there was a danger that spectators could leave you to sleep it off, and you would not get the help you needed. This would be potentially dangerous if you were suffering a severe low at the same time, with attendant risks of brain damage and death. Pretty good reasons why heavy drinking and diabetes should not be mixed.

Conversely, if I ate too much carbohydrate, I could go too high or hyperglycemic. While I may feel ok, if my blood sugar were high for long periods of time, it could damage my eyes, kidneys and nerves, and the risks of heart problems can shoot sky high. Even impotence can result. *Damn!* It seemed very sensible to strive for good diabetes control!

In the short-term, if blood sugars were running extremely high, my powers of concentration could be impaired. If blood sugars are very high and not treated, "ketoacidosis" can occur, possibly resulting in loss of consciousness and, ultimately, death. Ketoacidosis is dangerous but is much less common than hypos.

I learned to inject Regular insulin twice a day, 30 minutes before breakfast and 30 minutes before dinner. Each time I would mix 10 units of Regular (short-acting insulin) and NPH (longer-acting insulin). The short-acting insulin started to work about 45 minutes after injection and peaked around two hours later. The longer-acting insulin started acting after four hours and peaked anywhere between 6 and 8 hours. The short-acting covered breakfast and a mid-morning snack, while long-acting covered lunch and an afternoon snack. In the evening, short-acting would cover dinner and a bed-time snack, and long-acting would act while I was asleep. However, control was not always consistent. (On the vast majority of nights, I was fine. On a few, I would wake up feeling low. I am thankful that my warning symptoms were strong enough to wake me up, so I could recognize what was happening and eat some carbohydrate.) While I got general guidance, every person's insulin requirement was different, and over time, the number of insulin units injected could vary. I was told about a "honeymoon" period during which my pancreas could still be producing a low level of insulin for the first few months after diagnosis. If this happened, my insulin dosage would have to increase later on as the honeymoon gradually diminished.

I soon found that a mid-morning snack was vital to avoid going low. If breakfast was at 7:30 a.m., I would need a snack by 10 a.m., usually 30 g of low-fat, high-fiber biscuits. If I was "feeling" low (symptomatic), the quickest way to increase blood sugar was to eat candy (sweets) or drink fruit juice. Many people believe that you cannot eat sugar or anything sweet with diabetes. Certainly, people with type 2 diabetes who need to lose weight need to reduce sugary food intake, but if they take insulin, then they also need to be able to raise their blood sugar level quickly. Drinking fruit juice or eating candy is often the most effective way to prevent lows or raise blood sugars quickly if they are already low.

I had a long session with a dietician. I was supposed to eat a healthy, balanced diet, with roughly 60% of calories coming from carbohydrate, ideally eating higher-fiber foods so the glucose made from the digested carbohydrate was released slowly. Mixing carbohydrate with protein, such as meat or cheese, also slowed the release of glucose (sugar) into the bloodstream. Fruit and vegetables were a good source of carbohydrates. Eat less fat to reduce risks of heart disease. I have a sweet tooth and was worried about an appallingly boring diet. Sure, I had to cut out eating lots of bulk sugars such as chocolate bars and rich cakes at any one time. But overall, this was a healthy and reasonably varied diet. Not so bad really.

I was given a list of foods with the corresponding amounts of carbohydrate. This was my introduction to *carb counting,* a particularly powerful tool for managing diabetes and one I use to this day. A glass of milk has 12 grams (g) of carb, a slice of bread 15 g. I memorized various ones, particularly for foods that I liked. Later I learned about the *glycemic index,* a comparison of the speed that sugar is released from various foods compared against a slice of white bread. Basically, the higher the fiber in the food, the lower the glycemic index and the slower the release of glucose, which makes it a better food for smoothing out sharp blood sugar swings. I find the glycemic index another powerful dietary tool for managing diabetes.

Exchanges were another meal planning tool we discussed. If you want a small glass of orange juice with your meal instead of water, you could "exchange" it for one normal-sized potato in the meal. I could replace boring carbs with tastier ones, within reason. In fact, the techniques for including a variety of food choices offered more flexibility than I initially feared would be the case.

The dietician went into detail. In order to reduce saturated fat and reduce coronary disease risk, I should drink low-fat milk, peel the skin off chicken, avoid red meat (no pork crackling—*blast!*) and eat more fish. This high-carb, low-fat diet has recently been the subject of debate, particularly with the recent popularity of the Atkins diet and the South Beach Diet. Atkins argues that carbs are responsible for the current explosion in numbers of overweight and obese people, because humans were originally hunter-gatherers, living on high-protein, high-fat and unrefined carbohydrate diets. The focus is slowly shifting to those unrefined carbs. Fruits, vegetables, and whole grains are the healthiest choices for everyone, but are not the carbohydrates that most of us eat. Meanwhile Dr. Bernstein, author of *Dr. Bernstein's Diabetes Solution* advocates a low-carb diet with as little as 30 g per day for people with diabetes. He argues that this is the only way to normalize blood sugars at a consistent 87 mg/dl.

During stabilization of my blood sugars, the messages were clear. I would be responsible for managing my diabetes. Test blood sugars often, eat sensibly and exercise regularly. Be diligent and I could lead a normal life. I really wanted to work for this worthy goal.

First Low

I had my first low in the first week of stabilization. It was deliberately engineered, so I could learn to recognize my own symptoms. I was apprehensive but curious about going low for the first time. I received an insulin injection at the normal time but didn't eat afterward. After an hour and a half, I began to feel a bit odd. I developed a headache, a dull but distinct pressure around the whole skull. I began to sweat, feel anxious, and had very slight tremors (shaking) in my hands. The symptoms became more acute. Shortly afterward, a nurse gave me a glass of orange juice. It was delicious—my body was craving sugar. A few minutes later, I began to feel better. After around 10 minutes, I had fully recovered but felt slightly drained.

I believe that this exercise was an excellent idea. When I left hospital after stabilization, I felt reasonably confident that I could recognize hypoglycemia symptoms and do something about it.

In 1989, it was not possible to fly with insulin-dependent diabetes because of the risk of hypos and the potential for impaired judgment, incapacitation or passing out. Indeed, at that time, it was impossible to gain a flying license anywhere in the world.

Even now, with much improved insulin therapy and more advanced blood glucose monitoring, sadly, many careers remain banned for people with insulin-dependent diabetes. It varies from country to country and between some states in the U.S., but commonly, this restriction includes commercial flying, commercial driving (buses, trucks), fire services, military and police services. That means if you have insulin-dependent diabetes (or type 2 diabetes with medication that can result in hypoglycemia) your application will *automatically* be rejected. If you are diagnosed after your career is established, you may be able to continue but with restrictions. One example is the police services in the U.K., where a few years ago, a newly diagnosed person with insulin-dependent diabetes was able to continue in the force but was prevented from driving a police car or wearing firearms.

Several sports can also be restricted, including scuba diving in some countries, boxing, and of course, flying as a hobby. I remember gaining a PADI diving qualification in Thailand, but PADI in Malta would not allow me to dive. It can be an extremely frustrating situation, particularly when you have experience in such activities and don't have a problem managing your diabetes.

3 Taking Control

You are the best person to know what to do. You manage your own diabetes regime and know what works and what does not.
—Consultant Endocrinologist, London, 1991

The trick is what one emphasizes.
We either make ourselves miserable
Or we make ourselves strong.
The amount of work is the same....

—Carlos Castaneda

Life with Diabetes

It took about two months to begin building some confidence with managing diabetes. Chrissy and I adopted a lower fat diet. I counted carbs, eating them "in moderation." I experimented a bit with food intake, testing my blood sugars often after meals to find what the effect was and how predictable control could be. I had a few mild lows but within a few minutes of eating sweets or some form of rapidly absorbed carbohydrate (such as fruit candy or orange juice), I would be back to normal.

The first severe low took me by surprise. Richard Watson, a good RAF friend, was coming over for dinner and to stay the night. I injected 30 minutes before the anticipated mealtime, but Richard ended up being an hour late due to traffic. Shortly before he arrived, I developed a headache, felt shaky, nauseated and sweated profusely. This was much more intense than in hospital, and I took longer to return to normal after eating some sweets. Whenever anything unusual happens, I always want to learn something from it. What did I learn on this occasion? Don't take your insulin until you definitely know you're going to eat. Or if you have injected your insulin, snack on carbs until you can sit down for your delayed meal.

I tested my blood sugars a good four times a day, as recommended. I experimented with exercise, resuming jogs around my local neighborhood. I gradually built up distance each day, testing both before and after exercise to gauge the effect and to anticipate the lingering effects on my blood sugars over 24 hours.

I avoided alcohol for the first couple of months, leading to a regrettable incident. Jon May, a good old 63 Course (Basic Flying Training Course) mate, was planning his stag night on a ferry across the English Channel to France. It was to be a big drinking session, much as usual for our old basic flying course mates. However, I was in the early stages of getting used to diabetes and didn't feel confident about a drinking environment and a late night. With mixed feelings, I gave my apologies. I was upset when I learned just how much fun this stag party had been! I felt bad at missing Jon's stag party—he was a good friend. Had it been a couple of months later, I would have gone, even if I had not had any alcohol.

After a few months, I began to drink a small amount of wine and beer, and gradually built up my confidence. Whenever I drank alcohol, I was careful to test my blood sugars more often to make sure I wouldn't go low. By the time I moved to London, I found I could spend a highly spirited evening with friends. Some people later remarked that they would never have known I had diabetes unless I had told them.

The recommendation is to eat carbs along with any alcohol that you are drinking. I found that the carbohydrate in beer pushed my sugars up very fast, significantly exceeding the sugar-lowering effect of the alcohol. In 1996 I met a guy in Bangkok with type 1 diabetes who had an amazing physiology for drinking beer. The carbohydrate in Heineken beer *exactly* offset the blood sugar-lowering effect of the alcohol. He said he could literally drink till the cows came home—his blood sugar would be "exactly the same after ten pints."

I got used to taking candy *everywhere* I went. I would also try to remember to take my diabetes kit with me, even if going out for a short time. One time I forgot to pack my kit (insulin and blood glucose meter) for a weekend trip and had to survive for 36 hours without them. While my insulin worked for 10–12 hours on the first day, the rest of the time I was miserable trying to avoid carbohydrate and not knowing what my blood sugars were. They were pretty high by the time I got back home the next day. I vowed to try to be more organized in the future and always to take my kit with me wherever I went.

Looking back it's quite amazing that I wasn't referred by my general practitioner to an endocrinologist until a good year after diagnosis. If I'd had problems with control, no doubt, I'm sure I'd have gone sooner. Now I register with an endo as soon as I move anywhere new.

In the first few years, I was shy about testing glucose and injecting in public. I would always disappear into a restroom and do it in private. However, diabetes is an increasingly common condition, and while type 1 represents only 5–10% of total diabetes incidence, it is estimated that more than 30% of people with type 2 diabetes also inject insulin. Nowadays I test in public, although I'm sensitive to the people around me. I find insulin pens for injecting rapid-acting insulin work well. They look so much like a pen that people usually have no idea that you've just injected.

There seem to be parallels between flying and managing diabetes. Both require focused attention, with guidelines and rules to follow. They require vigilance and monitoring of instruments—blood glucose meters to confirm how good your control is, cockpit instruments to confirm flying accuracy. If you're outside normal parameters, you take action to regain control. Both require hard work. Certainly it was hard work to remember everything at first. But once I began to feel more familiar with the routine, it didn't seem to affect my day-to-day life significantly. It was a condition that just *had* to be controlled. It felt like I could essentially lead a normal life—except for flying, of course.

Motivation

An extremely important aspect of diabetes management is motivation. It's imperative to *want* to achieve good control in the first place. Very simply, I enjoy and am motivated by feeling fit and healthy. The best way to feel fit and healthy is to have good blood sugar control, and in turn, good blood sugar control is greatly helped by regular exercise and a healthy diet. It's a circular, positively reinforcing process.

I have come across a number of people who claim that the diagnosis of diabetes led to a healthier lifestyle and a better sense of well-being. Alternatively, I've met people who find the opposite is true, being frustrated with major changes to their diet and bitterly frustrated with poor control. It's extremely important to gain the knowledge and skills that can help you achieve good diabetes control. I was lucky to have learned from medical staff with excellent information when I was in hospital. It was extremely important during stabilization to learn that it is possible to control diabetes. Diabetes does not have to control you.

One quite shocking memory stands out from the stabilization time in hospital and acts to this day as a strong motivator. A 50-year-old farm laborer with diabetes was admitted to a private room suffering from gangrene of the leg. Having just read about the long-term possibility of neuropathy and wound infections deteriorating into gangrene and amputation, I went to his room, swallowed hard and entered. I wanted to chat with him. I had never seen or smelled gangrene before. I won't forget it. He had been at a dinner dance a few weeks earlier where his partner had stood on his foot with a sharp heel and punctured his skin. His blood sugar control had been poor for years. Soon afterward an infection developed, spreading up his foot to his leg and deteriorated into gangrene. Tragically he had neglected to visit a nurse or doctor as soon as the wound happened.

As I left the room, he made an emotional plea, shouting, "Don't do what I have done! I have neglected my diabetes for years, just carried on eating and ignoring high blood sugars. Make sure you look after yourself!" Two days later his leg was amputated below the knee. I will never forget what he said to me.

I am aware that every time my sugars are high, the likelihood of long-term complications is increased. If a result is high, I try to get the blood sugar down to normal as quickly as possible. I remember the plea from the farmer only too well. (I sometimes scratch the soles of my feet, appreciating the sensation I have and not suffering from neuropathy.) Setting my alarm and waking up in the middle of the night to test blood sugars can be a bother, but it's worth every *single* moment of effort to try to achieve good control.

I gained another motivational boost in Scotland in 2002 when I attended a talk by Dr. Andy Gallacher, a leading consultant diabetologist from

Victoria Infirmary, Glasgow. Dr. Gallacher suggested that since I had been diagnosed between 20–30 years of age, statistically I could only expect to live until 58. I can assure you that I want to live *a lot* longer than that. The best way to pass this age is to achieve good overall diabetes control. Over time, as insulin therapy continues to improve, the average lifespan figures should increase. Regardless, statistics like these act as a powerful incentive to work hard for good blood sugar control—to give myself the very best chance for good health.

So far I've remained motivated by myself to manage my diabetes (and I've been fortunate that my metabolism responds well to my control efforts), but many people find it difficult. I've learned that Denmark's diabetes association has come up with an excellent group motivational scheme. "Trainers" with type 2 diabetes are taught to lead groups of 10–12 people who meet together, learn how to exercise and to cook healthy meals with interesting recipes to improve their control. Results for the group have been tremendously encouraging with significant improvements in diabetes control. Most participants have enjoyed improved health and a renewed sense of well-being. From what I have seen, more groups like these are needed around the world.

A1C Tests

One of the most important things I learned after diagnosis was the importance of A1C tests, a measure of average blood sugar control over the previous three months. We are told to shoot for an A1C of 7% or lower, the level at which the chance of long-term complications are vastly reduced. A normal (non-diabetic) range is 4.3–5.8%. For every 1% reduction in A1C, we reduce the risk of long-term diabetes complications by 40%. Therefore, the closer my A1C is to a normal range, the happier I am.

Very basically, to achieve good control and A1Cs below 7%, I carry out the five tenets of diabetes control:

1. Calculate the amount of insulin to inject for the amount of food (carb) I'm about to eat.
2. Check my blood sugars frequently.
3. Exercise regularly.
4. Eat a moderate reduced-carb diet.
5. Visit my healthcare team every three months for regular checkups.

Insulin Injections

I have always used multiple injections. Before July 2003, I injected a mix of Regular and NPH insulin twice a day with top-ups of short-acting Regular insulin when necessary. With this regimen, I had to be extremely disciplined about eating snacks between meals (to prevent going low) and be careful about lows during the night. My A1Cs were consistently in the 6% range with a few high 5% readings and one at 7.2%. This was very encouraging, and in itself, fed my motivation to maintain good control.

Having an insulin pump was not an option for me in the U.K. They are expensive, between $4,000–$6,000. To qualify on the National Health Service, people had to have difficulty controlling diabetes with high A1Cs and frequent severe lows. Many people I have spoken with claim pumps are good to use and often result in "tighter" control. In the U.S., they are much more common, particularly among children. I can see definite advantages of using an insulin pump.

Now I inject glargine (Lantus) long-acting insulin once a day and inject rapid-acting (Humalog or Novolog) insulin for meals. Before each meal or snack, I work out how much carbohydrate I will eat and inject rapid-acting insulin to match—1 unit of insulin for each 10 grams of carbs. The insulin goes to work in 15 minutes or less to take care of the carbs and seems to be out of the system within a couple of hours.

Now that I have the dosages worked out for both Lantus and rapid-acting insulin, I find this regimen predictable and working well for me. Within six months of using this insulin combination, my A1Cs improved one full point to low 5.0% figures (my three-month check-up figures for 2004 were 5.0%, 5.4%, 5.3% and 5.3% respectively). Lantus seems to be stable, working for 24 hours without peaking. I can now sleep at night with significantly less concern about going low. (I recently went to sleep at 11 p.m. after a test result of 121 and woke up eight hours later with exactly the same figure.) While in Europe in 2003, I heard that the number of lows may be reduced when you change to Lantus from another longer-acting insulin. So far I have found this to be the case. I have been extremely impressed.

With improved A1Cs, fewer lows, being able to eat and sleep whenever I like, combining Lantus with rapid-acting insulin has given me a new taste of *freedom*.

They always say time changes things, but you actually have to change them yourself.

—Andy Warhol

Testing Blood Sugars

The common recommendation for people with type 1 diabetes is to test four times a day. However, research shows that more frequent testing results in better (tighter) control. I presently test at least eight times a day. This is very similar to the "8-point test plan" used by research teams in determining levels of control in the U.S. I test before each meal and also 1.5 hours after each meal (postprandial). I want to be somewhere between 72–126 mg/dl (4–7 mmol/l), a normal blood sugar range, but always calculate injections to achieve 80. According to Dr. Bernstein in his *Diabetes Solution* book, a normal (non-diabetic) figure is 87. Many people aim for 100, but I find using 80 works well for me.

Some people in the U.K. have looked at me in amazement because I test more often than the normal recommendation of four times a day. I have even been accused of being "obsessive." My response is simply to say, "Do whatever works to achieve good control." I can assure you, I am happy to be obsessive to ensure good daily control, avoid going low, and reduce or, perhaps, totally avoid the risk of debilitating complications. Everyone is different and what suits some will not suit others. Some find finger pokes painful and inconvenient for testing. I don't mind some short-term discomfort or inconvenience to achieve good control and good overall quality of life. For me a minimum of eight tests a day works extremely well.

It's a bit like driving in a speed zone of 30–50 mph in the U.S. The more often you check your speedometer the more likely you can remain within the speed limit. If we break the speed limit, we may be caught and fined. Diabetes is similar. However, the fine is suffering diabetes complications, such as kidney failure, blindness, neuropathy and impotence. Or severe lows. Looking at speedometers doesn't cost anything. A test strip costs around 80 cents a pop. Four extra tests per day costs an additional $1,460 per year. I believe it's worth every extra dollar and cent to help achieve good control. The financial and social cost of long-term diabetes complications far outweighs the short-term cost of four test strips a day.

It is worth noting that a number of companies are racing to bring continuous blood glucose monitoring to the market, particularly for people with insulin-dependent diabetes and children with diabetes. I cannot think of a better tool with which to achieve good blood sugar control. The more information we have at our fingertips (excuse the pun) the better. Ultimately, a "closed loop" insulin pump with continuous monitoring and automatic insulin delivery will result in a "mechanical cure." When such a pump is available, I dearly hope to use one.

Exercise

Another key ingredient for controlling diabetes is exercise. At the time of this writing, I normally jog or use a cycle-machine at least four times a week for 20 minutes. This seems to keep my metabolism ticking along and has clear aerobic benefits. Whatever the exercise, I make sure it's one I enjoy. If a pool is available, I'll swim every day. If a gym is unavailable and jogging is out of the question, I'll go for a brisk walk. After moving to Thailand and enjoying its beautifully warm (hot) climate, I began to swim every day, usually before breakfast and sometimes twice a day. It is a tremendously refreshing way to wake up, energize and prepare oneself for the day's work.

I find there is an excellent fringe benefit to physical exertion—endorphins. Exercising can give you a sense of well-being, even mild euphoria. See how you feel after a good swim or brisk walk or jog. It can be great. Not only that, you know that the exercise is doing you good. It's a positive spiral upward.

Exercise lowers blood sugar. So, I test my sugar beforehand, and if necessary, eat some rapidly absorbed carbohydrate to avoid going low during the exercise. I *always* carry carbs (candy) with me, however short the exercise session will be. I'm aware that exercise can lower blood sugars for up to 24 hours after finishing. I often find this is the case for about 12–18 hours afterwards.

I still thoroughly enjoy skiing and will take my blood glucose monitor and strips with me to test mid-morning, before lunch and mid-afternoon. It's easy to go low when skiing hard, so I'll take a decent amount of carbs with me. I'll also zip some fast-acting insulin into an inside pocket to ensure that it doesn't freeze.

If I'm swimming at the beach, I try to wear shorts that have a waterproof pocket for candy. The last place I'd want to go low is swimming 100 meters offshore when I know the swim back will lower blood sugar even further. I *always* test my sugar before swimming in the sea.

Sometimes if my sugar is high and time permits, I'll top up with a small amount of insulin *and* exercise. Recently I was frustrated to find my sugar was 232, having misjudged my lunchtime carb 1.5 hours earlier. I topped up with rapid-acting insulin and five minutes later, spent 16 minutes on a low-impact jogging machine. Precisely half an hour after the high reading, my blood sugar was 124, within a normal range. (I'll also test again within an hour, in case the after-effect of exercise is to go too low.) Some people find that if their blood sugar is very high, say 300, then exercise can raise it even further, but that has not been my experience.

If I don't exercise for a few days, I find my control deteriorates. Blood sugar levels become higher for the same insulin dosage. I have to increase my insulin dosage a little after a few days or reduce carbs. In October 2003, I tore a knee ligament and couldn't jog or even swim for almost three months. There was a noticeable deterioration in blood sugar control, resulting in my A1C increasing from 6.3% in October to 6.8% in December. I began exercising again in late December and (combined with an adjustment in Lantus dosage), two months later my A1C was down to 5.0%. From my experience over the last 16 years, daily exercise significantly helps my diabetes control.

Diet

When I was 25 years old, my "fighting weight" was about 11 stone or 154 pounds (71 kg). At that time, I could eat what I liked and stay the same weight. In retrospect it was bliss. A few years later, I gained weight quite easily if I was eating more or exercising less than usual—classic signs of aging.

When I tried to lose weight, I carefully reduced all food intake, including carbohydrates, and reduced insulin accordingly, while still eating a well-balanced diet. I also tried to exercise a little more than usual. The results were fascinating. In addition to losing weight, my blood sugar control was noticeably better. The swings up and down (roller coasters at times) were smoothed out. Many more blood sugar readings were within a normal range of 72–126 mg/dl. When I had reached my target weight loss, I would revert to my normal higher carbohydrate diet. Suddenly my blood sugar control wasn't as good, and I would put some weight back on. Before long I would return to a reduced-carb diet and repeat the process. Every time it was the same. For me, fewer carbohydrates meant improved diabetes control. The message was loud and clear. It made common sense to reduce overall carbohydrate intake to achieve better diabetes control.

I now eat a reduced-carb diet of around 80–100 g carbohydrates per day, less than is recommended on food labels, and around half of what I used to eat. I am sure this has helped achieve more stable blood sugar levels and A1Cs in the high 5% and mid 6% range in the last few years. In 2004 I used glargine with rapid-acting insulin, kept to a reduced-carb diet and continued to exercise regularly, and my A1Cs improved to low 5.0% figures. I am extremely happy with these results.

While my reduced-carb diet remains healthy and balanced, I augment my diet with a daily multivitamin pill plus an olive oil pill with garlic, rich in omega-3 fat, which is an anti-inflammatory—good for heart and blood vessels. I find this useful, particularly when I am traveling, and my diet is not so consistent.

I find it's impossible to be disciplined *all* the time. If I'm feeling a bit down about something, or simply extremely hungry, sometimes I can't resist a piece of cake, candy, or a larger meal than normal—an "eating binge." I guess it's just human nature. I will try to offset a binge by injecting more rapid-acting insulin. However, the carbohydrate in sweet food (white flour and refined sugar) is absorbed quickly, and I've gone high on occasions after indulging.

The potential benefits of a reduced-carb diet were demonstrated recently by two people I know. Steph Speer, a 17 year old from California, lost four pounds late in 2003 by reducing her carbs and found that her A1C improved from 11 to 9%. When I spoke with her, she was really fired up about her reduced-carb diet and improving her diabetes control further. A good friend in Omaha, Dave Geiger, who has type 2 diabetes, recently adopted a reduced-carb diet (a mixture of the Atkins and the South Beach Diet) and found his regular blood sugar tests falling from an average of 140–160 to a steady 70 for almost every single test. He was impressed. So was I.

During Diabetes World Flight, I was fascinated to meet Ron Raab, an International Diabetes Federation (IDF) vice president and founder of

Insulin for Life charity in Melbourne, Australia. Ron has had type 1 diabetes for 47 years, and until a few years ago, he had been unable to get good control and was suffering some debilitating long-term complications. He was getting desperate. Then he discovered *Dr. Bernstein's Diabetes Solution,* which recommended eating 30 g carbohydrate a day. Ron made his carb target 60 g in a range of 45–75 g (he found 30 g daily too restrictive) and significantly improved his blood sugar control as a result. Continuing this practice arrested the complications and reversed most of them over the following years. His quality of life has improved greatly. I understand why he is a strong advocate of using lower-carb diets to help normalize blood sugars, improve control and in many cases, improve quality of life. (Ron posts details of lower-carb diets on www.diabetes-low-carb.org.)

After finishing DWF, I decided to read both *Dr. Bernstein's Diabetes Solution* and *Dr. Atkins New Diet Revolution.* While both have been described as controversial, I found them interesting and educational. More recently I read *The South Beach Diet* written by a cardiologist who aims to reduce heart disease. It seems to be neither a low-carb nor a low-fat diet. It does, however, suggest an overall reduction of carbs, while exchanging "bad" carbs for "good" carbs (those with higher fiber). I was interested to find that my own reduced-carb diet was quite similar to the South Beach Diet.

I am extremely grateful to have met Ron Raab and to learn more about lower-carb diets. I now have some powerful new tools to use in managing my diabetes. I can make more informed decisions. It's all part of the empowering process of people with a chronic disease. However, what suits some may not suit others. It's "horses for courses" as we say in the U.K.

It's interesting to note that 10,000 years ago, our diet was 65% protein and fat (as outlined by Dr. Loren Cordain in *The Paleo Diet*), and relatively little carbohydrate. As agriculture developed over the millennia, cereal crops grew in importance, and the amount of carbohydrates eaten gradually increased from 35% to 60% of our diet. Recommending that people reduce carbs (and conversely increase relative amounts of protein and fat in our diet) would be quite a change of mindset for many diabetes associations and health services. It will take time for research to provide conclusive evidence of the benefits (or otherwise) of reduced-carb diets. In the meantime, I will continue practicing what works extremely well for me in managing my diabetes—a diet with 100 g carbs or less a day.

Hypos or Lows

I have been very fortunate so far to avoid major problems with hypos. I have excellent warning systems at present, feeling shaky and sweaty at first and "slightly strange." I can also feel a bit irritable, something I hate. Normally I can detect these symptoms early and eat readily absorbable carbohydrate (candy), or drink something sweet like regular Coke to bring sugars back up. Sugar is not absorbed in the stomach but in the small intestine. The quicker it gets there the better, so a sweet drink is effective. I've been told that even the natural sugar in milk is appropriate for this, too.

If my sugar is lowering very slowly, or I'm tired and/or I've been drinking alcohol, I may miss these first symptoms. Normally, however, the next symptom is a tiny gold patch that appears in my line of vision, similar to an impression of a powerful light or even sunshine suddenly hitting you in the eye. I then know I'm quite low, perhaps 50 mg/dl. If I don't eat candy straight away, this tiny light can spread into a larger orb. When I eat candy or take a sweet drink, about 30 seconds later, the golden patch disappears.

Another symptom of hypoglycemia for me is feeling anxious. Sometimes I feel worried, even mildly depressed, for instance, about issues to do with work or a project I may be doing. When I was working in Thailand, I could wake up in the middle of the night feeling anxious about being so far away from home in the U.K. Within a few minutes of eating candy, my anxiety would disappear as if by magic.

I have been quite frightened a few times. Without exception, scary moments have coincided with drinking alcohol and burning the midnight oil too much—that is, being tired. In Australia one night after returning from a wedding reception, I tested before going to bed. I had injected myself with short-acting insulin about 1.5 hours earlier, and I felt symptoms of being low. Well, I definitely was low, at 40 mg/dl. I suspect my fatigued state and steady alcohol intake that day had masked some of my normal early warning symptoms such as shakiness or sweating.

I ingested 20 g carbs and retested 15 minutes later. This was more than the standard "15/15 rule" of ingesting 15 g carb and testing again 15 minutes later. But the next test figure was even lower. I ingested another 20 g carbs and tested twice more before bottoming out at 29 and rising again. Alcohol blocks the liver from releasing glycogen/sugar into the bloodstream, and the body loses part of its automatic response to low blood sugar, which is releasing adrenaline and other hormones to raise blood sugars. I have found on a few occasions that alcohol masks some of my hypo warning symptoms. I am more careful about alcohol intake these days.

Another time I was worryingly low was on a ski holiday. I had been skiing energetically for a week with lots of late nights and a steady intake of alcohol. One night a few of us suddenly decided to go out late, and in the rush, I forgot to test my blood sugar. Shortly afterward, I suddenly felt *very* low. Alcohol and fatigue had masked the early warning symptoms. By the time I recognized I was low and stuffed candy into my mouth, I was feeling truly awful.

I hate hypos with a passion. I'm scared of them. I really don't want to endanger my life with a seizure and end up in hospital—not now or ever, if I can possibly help it. This is one reason why I test my blood sugars frequently. It's the best way to detect lows and do something—ingest sugar—before it gets dangerously low.

Influence

Some people have influenced and greatly assisted my diabetes management. In the first instance, the healthcare team during stabilization acted as a strong and positive influence. I was lucky to receive and have good advice over the 10 days I was in hospital. After reading the two books, I had many follow-up questions to ask. The dietician's advice was invaluable, particularly on how to count carbs while making a diet healthy and interesting.

Over the past year, *Dr. Bernstein's Diabetes Solution* has had a positive effect. In addition to learning about potential benefits of a reduced-carb diet, I learned some finer points about diabetes management, such as how to get quicker uptake of insulin by injecting directly into upper forearm muscle instead of into subcutaneous fat on the stomach or not injecting more than 8 units in one site. More can reduce the consistency of insulin absorption. I now divide my current once daily dose of longer-acting insulin into four separate injection sites. Okay, this might seem like more unwanted injections, but if it may give more consistent control, I am happy to do this.

Sonia Cooper, President of the Children with Diabetes Foundation, has profoundly influenced my diabetes management of late. Her son, Matthew, was diagnosed at the age of two, and she launched herself wholeheartedly into the diabetes community. She now works with Dr. Peter Chase at the Barbara Davis Center for Childhood Diabetes in Denver, focusing on research while raising funds for research and supporting important developments in the industry. Her knowledge of diabetes is impressive. It was Sonia who persuaded me to change to glargine long-acting insulin in combination with rapid-acting insulin at meals. Once I got the dosage right, it felt like total freedom. I can now eat when I like, and sleep happier—worrying significantly less about about going low during the night. Moreover, my A1Cs have improved to low 5% figures. I appreciate having more predictable control, fewer mild hypos and greater freedom.

Finally, Ron Raab articulated for me what a low-carb diet really is. Ron is a remarkable man, dedicated to diabetes and diet awareness and runs a tremendous charity called Insulin For Life (IFL). IFL collects and sends insulin, syringes and blood glucose meters to disaster relief areas around the world, usually third world countries in desperate need. Ron and his team save peoples' lives.

> *A wise man should consider that health is the greatest of human blessings, and learn how by his own thought to derive benefit from his illnesses.*
>
> —Hippocrates

Chapter:

4 A New Career, A New Life

What Next?

In September 1989, I handed my RAF identity card in to the RAF Linton-on-Ouse guardhouse, climbed into my car and drove 200 miles to London to start a new career. I had intensely mixed feelings. It was seven months since being diagnosed with diabetes. I was leaving my old career and life behind. While the RAF had offered me a change of branch from flying to administration or supply, I felt I didn't really have any choice—I had joined the RAF to fly. Working "on the ground" in the RAF, I would have felt terribly frustrated. I had to move on to a new and, hopefully, challenging career. Finance was my new chosen career, but there was a major difference. I would have to "work for a living," flying a Mahogany Mark II office desk rather than an exciting Jet Provost TMark5.

The RAF was good to me in my last six months prior to leaving. I remained with my training squadron at RAF Linton-on-Ouse, teaching ground school while applying for jobs in "civvy street." About six weeks after diagnosis, I went flying with colleagues. Each time I tested my blood sugar before climbing into the cockpit, and then my colleagues would usually let me have the controls for a good part of the following hour, flying formation, low flying and general handling (steep turns, stalls, aerobatics). It occurred to me that if diabetes were well controlled, it should be safe to fly. It was a bittersweet experience. It was tremendous to be flying but painful to be reminded that it was something I loved yet wasn't allowed to do.

One aspect of RAF life that could have tempted me to stay was the skiing. I could have gained up to two months of skiing every year in Europe and Australia on duty. During the last six months in the RAF, I managed the annual British Combined Services Ski Team trip to Australia, and my final three weeks of active duty were spent skiing in Australia. Being so busy and flying from time to time with squadron colleagues blocked out the grim reality of my imminent departure from the RAF.

In many respects, my decision to start a career in finance was logical. I had enjoyed business studies courses at University, particularly Finance that seemed both interesting and challenging. After researching various options, I applied for graduate recruit/training courses in corporate finance and fund management, plus management consulting. Several companies had rejected my applications. Most applicants were 20 or 21 years of age. At 26, I could have been regarded as too old for graduate training courses, making it difficult to mold a crusty old guy like me into an ideal employee. Some may not have liked the military background.

One great thing about the U.K. is that my geography degree did not hinder applications for a finance career. The degree was a passport to interviews, and if I were selected, I would attend a graduate-training scheme of around three months before "learning on the job." This system does not exist in many countries, such as the U.S. and Australia, where a business career invariably requires a business or relevant degree or experience.

Chrissy was from Australia, so we considered moving to Sydney. Three months after diagnosis, I traveled to Sydney on Japan Airlines. It was my first long-haul flight with diabetes, and I followed the travel advice of my doctor, including a request for "diabetic meals" on flights. I had injected approximately 30 minutes before the first meal and was horrified to be served one measly bit of bread as the only carbohydrate. *Where were the Japanese noodles?*

Where was the rice? I desperately needed more carbs and had to ask for another two rolls to avoid going low. I have *never* ordered a special diabetic meal since. I always eat normal meals on flights.

It was a busy 10 days in Australia, and I was delighted to receive an offer from management consulting firms McKinsey & Company and LEK Partnership. However, it did not feel right. Originally Chrissy and I had agreed to move to Australia at the end of my RAF permanent commission—13 years later. It seemed too soon to be leaving the U.K.

When I met Chrissy at London Heathrow Airport, before I could say anything, she quietly said that it felt too soon to move to Australia. It was quite remarkable that we both felt the same way. A couple of months later, I was offered a job with an American bank in London as a Research Associate in the Corporate Finance Department, specializing in Leveraged Buyouts (LBOs). LBOs were all the rage in the late 80s, described as stimulating and challenging work, key descriptive words that I'd been using during interviews. However, dark clouds of recession loomed over the horizon in 1989. Dark clouds also loomed on the personal horizon.

A New Career In Finance

My new job was in corporate finance involving background industry research, detailed company financial analysis, working out future prospects and values for companies with a view to management taking them over—management buyouts.

I knew that good diabetes control would ensure a good chance of establishing a new career. I continued with frequent blood sugar testing (usually disappearing into the office toilet for privacy), a moderate diet and plenty of exercise. Over the following months, it was good to see stable control while settling into the new job and life in London.

After one year, I joined a senior colleague, Hans Wackwitz, and specialized in European airlines. Much of the work was getting to know airlines, their fleets and identifying aircraft leasing opportunities. It was interesting stuff, and it involved airplanes. Hans was a Dutchman, and the Scots and Dutch have the same reputation for being miserly with their money. (It was a good combination!) Unfortunately the finance industry recession that began in 1989 dragged into the early 90s, and aircraft leasing opportunities dried up for any newcomers to the sector, including us. In February 1991, I was made redundant.

Despite this setback, I knew exactly what I wanted to do. I had found my attention increasingly drawn to the stock market. During RAF training, a few of us had traded shares. I only made money once, but I found this "calculated gambling" almost addictive. I had already applied to Schroder Investment Management in London in 1989, but it was too late to join their graduate-training course. I re-applied in 1991, and after a rigorous set of interviews was offered a job. I was delighted. Fund management seemed a fascinating area of finance, and Schroders was a fast-growing, highly regarded company.

My new job at Schroders was to analyze the breweries and distilleries sectors of the U.K. stock market, along with the leisure and entertainment sector. Hmmm! This sounded like drinking and being entertained for a living— not bad at all! Thus began an extremely enjoyable and fulfilling 11-year career with Schroders. I spent 18 months as an analyst before progressing on to U.K. equity pension fund management. After four years at Schroders, I was managing $800 million (U.S.) of assets for 20 clients. There was a vibrant and positive atmosphere, and my colleagues were a great bunch of people, many of whom have become good friends.

It is interesting to note that fund management requires discipline within a fascinating and challenging work environment. This had some parallels to RAF flying. I was back to a meaningful career that I enjoyed. Overall it was *fun*. That was worth a million dollars. There is no doubt that luck plays its hand in anyone's career. I was definitely lucky to find a second career that I genuinely enjoyed.

Unsettling Times

While I was lucky to establish an enjoyable and rewarding second career after two years, the route toward it was rife with pressures, strains and roller-coaster emotional swings. I had to start at my first job at the very bottom rung of a career ladder again, as junior as could be. Although I had accepted this situation, it remained difficult to adjust after being a flying instructor in the RAF. The atmosphere in the RAF had been competitive but an overall camaraderie prevailed. The atmosphere in London was also competitive but had sporting (occasionally vicious) office politics to play. There was little in the way of camaraderie, undoubtedly a function of trying business conditions. At times the work was interesting, but I couldn't help comparing it to flying and finding it terribly bland. My boyhood dream had never been to work in a bank corporate finance department! I remember looking out of my window one day and noting gray buildings all around, not one single scrap of green vegetation anywhere. It certainly wasn't the same as my old JP5 "office" at 3,000 feet with its exhilarating, high-speed views of England's beautiful countryside.

Meantime Chrissy and I had settled into London life, spending time with new and old friends, skiing in the Alps during winter, and traveling to Australia every 18 months to see Chrissy's family. Jon and Fiona May, very good RAF friends who were then living in London, thought that we had a golden life. We had good jobs at multinational companies, enjoyed an active social life and had great holidays. However, deep down I was grieving for a lost flying career. In public I put on a brave face. In private it was another matter.

One month after starting my new job, I attended an accountancy course in Hammersmith in west London. On a cold, wet and windy afternoon I watched a commercial DC-10 passenger jet break out of cloud on its approach into Heathrow Airport. My heart fell in line with the aircraft's descent. With a sudden jolt I realized just how much I was missing flying and the RAF. *That* was where I wanted to be, *up there* in that jet. Not here on the ground with boring old accountancy! These particular thoughts triggered a clinical depression that lasted almost 18 months.

In retrospect I should have sought medical help. People with diabetes have a relatively high propensity for depression, adjusting to a life-altering and potentially life-threatening condition. I had also lost my dream career. Chrissy knew that I was depressed, and it was terribly hard on her. She had previously known a positive guy who loved his career and his life. All that had changed. Depression began to show through and my behavior affected our relationship, our great friendship and partnership.

It was a desperately unsettling time. In many respects I tried to deny what I was going through. There were aspects of my job I didn't feel confident with. I was particularly anxious about a career I didn't enjoy and saw no future in. Meantime I just couldn't think of anything that I *really* wanted to do. It was impossible to stop myself being wistful about my old career. Within a year I was hunting for a new job and a new career. At one point, I thought seriously about trying to get back into the RAF in a ground job. But I reached the same conclusion as before; this would have been a terrible idea. I'd have been constantly reminded of what I wanted to do most and couldn't. I would have stared wistfully out office windows at the aircraft I so wanted to fly. I thought about starting my own business. I was a 27-year-old married man, and there were times when I felt I couldn't live up to my responsibilities.

There were nights when falling asleep was a welcome relief. But the morning was like waking up to a bad dream, a grim reality where spirits plummeted. Even watching a good television program or a film could feel like brief respite from reality. One weekend I remember driving up from London to Dumfries, Scotland, to visit my sister, Ann, and her husband, Charlie. It was a cold winter's day in Dumfries and a warm fire was glowing. We watched a James Bond movie on the Saturday evening in a cozy, comfortable atmosphere. I looked at my sister and her husband, both doctors, and thought how lucky they were to have established careers that they seemed passionate about.

My sister once quietly said that losing a flying career was like suffering a family bereavement—a major loss. (When I was diagnosed, she said emotionally, "Why Dougie? Why not me with a career in medicine that diabetes should not affect!") I was mired in misery at times. I am thankful that my depression did not affect my immediate desire to manage my diabetes. I retained a desire to be fit and healthy, but it felt like there was no way out of this terribly negative frame of mind and somber spirit. I tried to put on a brave face with friends and colleagues but felt like an imposter. In reality, my confidence was shattered.

When redundancy came in February 1991, it was a relief. I now *had* to find an alternative job. It was an opportunity to make a new start. My new job at Schroders in April 1991 was a breath of fresh air. The work was interesting, I was gaining analytical skills in a specialized area, and the atmosphere in the research department was competitive while positive and cooperative. Plenty of banter flew around, and there was noticeable camaraderie. My depression began to lift. However, it had been an extremely unsettling time for Chrissy and me. We attended marriage counseling. Very sadly, two years later we parted company.

Move to Asia

Whenever I had traveled through Asia in my 20s, I'd found it fascinating—colorful, varied and vibrant. In late 1994, 18 months after splitting up with Chrissy, I went on holiday to Hong Kong and while there, spent three days in the local Schroders office. I found it captivating. When I returned to London, I had a chat with our department head and let him know that I was interested in working in Asia.

Five months later I discovered that a challenging new job was available in Bangkok, Thailand. The following day I ran up two floors to the company CEO's office and volunteered for the position. His response was great: "We were just about to ask you." In October 1995, I went to Bangkok for a recon (recce) trip. The city was loud, hot, congested, dusty, totally manic and in the middle of a frantic economic boom. It was exciting but stressful.

When I returned to London I thought, "I must be mad to be leaving my life here." In 1995, my spirits were higher. I was enjoying work and had a great set of friends in and around London. I was involved with the British Ski Club for the Disabled, running the training program for guiding disabled skiers and enjoying the company of fun-loving, enthusiastic people. I had started to see Helen, and we had a good relationship. I was happy with life in London.

Indeed, I felt apprehensive before leaving for Thailand. In the U.K., I was a "plain vanilla" fund manager whereas in Thailand, my role would be Chief Investment Officer, responsible for building up and managing a team of research analysts and fund managers covering the whole investment market. I suddenly had to make new friends and a new life in Bangkok, a frenetic, mad city 6,000 miles from home. However, I was willing to take the risk of stepping into the unknown, excited at the prospect of living in a new culture and taking on new responsibilities.

Managing Diabetes in Thailand

One vital issue to deal with before moving was how to manage my diabetes in Thailand. There was no easy way to find out which insulin was available, or where I could find a good doctor and endocrinologist. I also wondered how Thai food would affect control. Nowadays it's so much easier to find such information via the internet and contact with groups such as www.childrenwithdiabetes.com and www.diabetes.org.

On the first of two "recce trips" to Thailand in 1995, I paid a visit to Chulalongkorn Public Hospital. *Big mistake!* Hundreds of local people were milling around the corridors, chattering away in a foreign language I had absolutely no clue about. All the department signs were in Thai writing (a mixture of Greek and Chinese script), and I could only find one person who spoke English. Even after gaining directions, I found myself waiting for ages with nothing happening. It was terribly frustrating. Anyone I spoke with could not understand my English. From such chaos, I could never have imagined that Thailand would help inspire a dream to fly around the world.

I left the public hospital in defeat and battled the traffic to visit Bumrumgrad private hospital the next day. (By the way, Bumrumgrad hospital also has a good reputation for performing sex-change operations.) The signs were in English—*fantastic!* Most of the staff could speak some English, and overall the service was excellent. I soon saw a doctor who explained that my insulin and blood test strips were readily available. Moreover the company health insurance would cover the costs. It was a *tremendous* relief to find this out.

As with starting work in London, I knew that good diabetes control was vital for my work and progress in Thailand. Once I moved to Bangkok, I tested at least six times a day. However, some new food dishes surprised me. A favorite, chicken with cashew nuts, was sometimes laced heavily with sugar. Some unexpectedly high blood sugar readings followed, and it took me a few months to estimate more accurately how much carbohydrate would be in each dish—some good old carb-counting skills came in handy. Indeed, many dishes in Thailand can be laced with sugar or coconut, itself very high in carb. Whenever I had an unexpectedly high reading, I would top-up with short-acting insulin. If time permitted and it was convenient, I would also exercise soon after topping up to reduce sugars more quickly. Even though I had traveled extensively with diabetes, I was pleased to find my diabetes control continued well.

I wondered if the hot climate would affect blood sugar control and later learned that heat makes the heart pump faster and can increase insulin uptake. There were times when I found blood sugars lowered faster than expected when I was physically active in hot weather. However, I didn't notice any significant change in overall control, probably because I spent most of my working time indoors in cool air-conditioning. Indirectly, however, the hot climate did have an impact. Most apartment blocks I stayed at had a swimming pool, and I would always swim at least once a day. This regular exercise undoubtedly helped my diabetes control.

Life in Thailand

Thailand is known as "the country of smiles" where people are fun loving, friendly and relaxed. The expression "Mai pen rai" (don't worry, relax) is used often. Thai people can have a mischievous spirit, with great propensity for teasing people. Much of Thailand's countryside is stunning. To the west and north of Bangkok's central plains lie jungle-covered mountains that border Burma (Myanmar) and Laos. To the south are stunning beach resorts including the islands of Koh Samui and Phuket (which suffered tragic loss of life and devastation from the tsunami wave of 26 December 2004). Vietnam is less than an hour's flight to the east. It's an exceptional base from which to explore Asia, and I took full advantage of this.

If you're an active sportsman, Thailand has great appeal. There are more than 30 championship golf courses in the vicinity of Bangkok. Half an hour from Bangkok city center is a water skiing cable-tow park that groups of us would frequently visit. The beach resorts were easy to reach for weekends, and invariably had excellent diving facilities. (And Thailand's diving association allowed people with type 1 diabetes to dive.) I loved the change from chilly and damp winter U.K. weather to Thailand's warmth and sunshine. Even during the rainy season (late May until October), it is often sunny in the morning with short and sharp electrical storms in the afternoon or evening.

I had much to learn about Thai culture. High emotions and anger can be commonplace in Western offices but in predominantly Buddhist Thailand, a raised voice and anger is a sign of poor breeding and character. The Chinese concept of "losing face" could be a tricky issue to deal with at times, with some people tempted to hide a mistake or to try to take the easiest (and not necessarily the optimal) solution to a problem. Life isn't made any easier by a propensity for people to be indirect when confronting issues. People can sometimes "take the long winding path to reach the destination." Also behavior seen as corrupt in Westerners' eyes was, at times, prevalent in Thailand, and for many expatriates and locals, difficult to accept.

I was the only Westerner in our joint venture office and despite English being the official language, colleagues would naturally speak in Thai except during meetings. I learned enough Thai for basic conversations—enough to order a beer at least. I suspect there were many times when my Thai colleagues thought I was quite odd, and my decisions may not have been popular. There were times when I kicked myself hard for being too *farang* (Western) by showing anger or frustration. Every time I had an outburst, I felt I'd let myself down and resolved not to show my feelings again. It took time to improve. I was always far from perfect.

When I arrived, I was apprehensive about how things would progress with the new company set-up. I worked hard, eager to make it work well. Work days often stretched into late evening. Dinner at 10 p.m. was quite common even though I worked just 10 minutes from my apartment. Many weekends required work also. Having documents in both English and Thai involved huge amounts of proofreading. On a couple of occasions, I sat at my desk, head in hands, wishing I were back in the relative sanity of London. However, in the first 10 months, we achieved much, recruiting an excellent team and gaining a license to start up a mutual fund management joint venture company.

The business atmosphere in Bangkok was vibrant when I arrived. Thailand was a developing country and had enjoyed several years of uninterrupted economic growth. However, the following six years were not what I expected. Just 18 months after I arrived, the Thai Baht currency suddenly devalued by 50% and in turn, triggered an Asia-wide economic crisis. More than 40 finance companies were closed down by the government, leading to hundreds of construction companies grinding to a halt as they lost access to loan funding. Dozens of partially built tower blocks littered Bangkok's skyline. Thailand's domestic economy contracted by over 10% in 1998.

It was a volatile, stressful, yet exciting time to be in Thailand. There is probably no better experience than working through a boom and bust, and surviving. Our major bank partner and three smaller joint venture partners went bust and ultimately Schroders increased its original 25% stake to 80% and took control. I was eventually promoted to Chief Executive Officer in 2001. However, when our major bank partner was sold to an international bank, we suddenly lost our sole selling agent. It was difficult to build decent market share. In January 2002, Schroders sold its 80% stake, and my work contract finished.

Despite occasional frustrations, my six years working in Thailand were an immensely enjoyable and fulfilling period of my life. I would do it all over again.

Traveling

After moving to Thailand, I took at least four flights a year to the U.K. and had to get used to frequent long-distance traveling. The flight from Bangkok to London is about 12 hours, usually overnight, and has a seven-hour time difference. More recently, I made seven long-haul flights between Thailand, the U.K. and the U.S. in just two months, dealing with up to 15 time zones in one go. At the end of this marathon period, I was delighted to see my A1C at 5.0%, and there were no problems with hypos. (People often say that such low A1Cs must be accompanied by more frequent hypos. I have not found this to be the case so far with using Lantus and Humalog/Novolog combined with frequent blood sugar testing.)

Basically I follow four rules when traveling: 1) Eat slightly fewer carbs, 2) Test blood sugars more frequently, 3) Always have sufficient carbohydrate foods available and 4) *Always* keep diabetes supplies (insulin, syringes, blood glucose meter and test strips) in my hand luggage. I never put my diabetes supplies in a suitcase that goes into the baggage hold. I've had quite a few suitcases get lost in transit, and they can take *days* to be delivered. Big trouble if this happens with your diabetes kit packed inside. Also it's too cold in the baggage hold for your insulin.

When I'm sitting on a long-haul flight, aerobic exercise is impossible. I find that eating or drinking slightly fewer carbs than my daily average of around 100 g helps control. Eating slightly less seems to avoid some high and low blood sugar swings. I have, however, been caught wrong-footed with new foods in different countries, but testing frequently seems to help me avoid being too high for long. It also helps me anticipate going low. Whenever traveling abroad, I still try to exercise regularly. Jogging is a great way to explore new neighborhoods. If staying in hotels, I'll use a gym and swimming pool, if available.

Before I traveled for the first time, I took detailed advice from my doctor. It's extremely important to know how to deal with changing time zones and work out how to delay or advance or tweak multiple injections to achieve good control. (Active self-management at its best.) Nowadays, if I'm away for only a few days, I'll stay on "home" time. If traveling for longer periods, I will try to amend my Lantus injection to the local morning time, sometimes waking myself every two hours at night, testing and topping-up with rapid-acting insulin until I can take Lantus in the morning. I've often thought about the benefits of using an insulin pump while traveling. You wouldn't need to worry about delaying long-acting insulin injections. The pump delivers small amounts of rapid-acting insulin at a slow rate all the time, 24 hours a day, 7 days a week, providing the basal or background insulin that the body needs.

Over time I've become familiar with tweaking my diabetes management while traveling. At times it is hard work and requires considerable memory prompting. But as with everyday life, it's worth every single bit of effort to strive for good control.

> *Accuracy means something to me. It's vital to my sense of values. I've learned not to trust people who are inaccurate. Every aviator knows that if mechanics are inaccurate, aircraft crash. If pilots are inaccurate, they get lost—sometimes killed. In my profession life itself depends on accuracy.*
>
> —Charles A. Lindbergh

Chapter:

5 Flying Solo with Diabetes

If one advances confidently in the direction of his dreams, and endeavors to live the life which he has imagined, he will meet with a success unexpected in common hours.....If you have built castles in the air, your work need not be lost; that is where they should be. Now put the foundations under them.

—Henry David Thoreau

The Passion Remains

All throughout my new career, the passion to fly remained. It was, however, subdued for the first few years. I sometimes visited flying clubs near London, grabbing an instructor to act as a safety pilot and flying small planes like a Cessna 172 or Piper Cherokee. It was never the same as flying a jet, but it was tremendous to be airborne and blow some cobwebs away. It was also a relief to find I could still land an airplane, albeit rattling a few of the instructors' dentures.

Twice I flew in a high-performance aerobatic Pitts Special at White Waltham's grass airstrip even though the cost was prohibitive (clearly an issue for a Scotsman). Flying loops, stall turns, slow rolls and flick maneuvers over Berkshire's beautiful farmland was terrific, just like old days. It was always a mixed experience though. I was incredibly happy to fly each time but frustrated and depressed to get back on the ground, knowing I couldn't do this as a desired career.

Each time I flew, I tested my blood sugar shortly before takeoff and always took plenty of carbohydrate with me in the cockpit. I would chew on some sweets after half an hour if I thought my blood sugar was dropping. I never had any lows while flying. It was food for thought—I was confident that flying was safe with diabetes if I was sensible and disciplined. Had I known that I would be able to fly in the U.S. a few years later and could carry out a world flight, I would have been extremely excited. But I also would have been quite incredulous. In the early 90s, aviation authorities seemed vehemently opposed to anyone flying with diabetes.

At one stage, I dabbled in some aerial photography. It was really an excuse to get me flying. I snapped away with a large camera while leaning out the window of a Cessna 172, 500 feet above Berkshire's countryside. I marked the track on a map, and later matched photos up with houses along the route. At the end of each flight, I would take the controls for landing, a tremendous way to finish off.

I quite enjoyed selling photos on a few Saturdays. I came across some stunning properties and met a few of England's landed gentry. My sale strike rate was 25% (one sale for every four calls) and as a tiny part-time project, it proved marginally cash generative and profitable. Overall it was *fun* to combine some flying with photography this way.

On other occasions, I'd go flying on an opportunistic basis. After a new business presentation in Leeds, I had two hours to kill before flying back to London, so I nipped over to the Leeds/Bradford Airport flying club and went up in a Cessna 152 Aerobat with an instructor. Pulling loops, barrel rolls and stall turns was a great way to finish a working day! During the short flight, I saw my old base in the distance. A fleeting thought passed by, that one day it would be great to fly my own aircraft over the same airspace. Little did I know that nine years later I would do exactly this with a U.S. pilot's license.

Not long after leaving the RAF and moving to London, I contacted the Civil Aviation Authority to see if there might be developments to allow people with diabetes to fly. The elderly medic I spoke with was sympathetic and felt that while yes, there were people who could be well controlled, it would take many years before they would be allowed to gain a medical. He did, however, encourage me to keep in touch every couple of years.

A few years later, I spoke to a different guy. It was a depressing experience. He made it quite clear during our conversation that I was wasting his time, outlining that the likelihood of people flying with insulin-dependent diabetes was, in his opinion, zero. I was distressed when his assistant was also disparaging about people flying with diabetes. I was only too aware that if I lost it, or got angry, little help or consideration would ever be offered. It was best to be positive and constructive in any approach, and try to work *with* the authorities rather than against them. Unfortunately the second medic was aggressive and, without meaning to be, was quite insulting in his approach. (If someone is being defensive, perhaps it is easier to miss how insulting comments can be.) That was in the 1990s. Fortunately things have changed positively since then. It is now possible for me to fly in four countries, the U.S., U.K., Australia and Canada. However, the U.S. is the only country that allows full, unrestricted private-licensed flying.

Flying in Thailand

> *Flying may not be all plain sailing, but the fun of it is worth the price.*
>
> —Amelia Earhart

In my first year in Asia, I only flew once in Thailand and once in New Zealand. However, from 1997 onward I flew often. Indeed, flying in Thailand proved to be a Scotsman's delight, being less than half the cost of London flying clubs. I befriended a highly spirited Yorkshireman, Gillem, who had a U.K. flying license and 80 hours total-time to his name. We were soon flying at Ratchaburi, a tiny flying club 100 miles from Bangkok.

Ratchaburi province has stunning mountains to the west on the Burmese border, with lowland rice paddies studded with limestone karsts rising hundreds of feet sheer out of the ground. I flew with Group Captain Jira, a retired Thai Air Force instructor, and sometimes with Gillem. Jira was an extremely cheerful guy and had flown tiny bombers at treetop height in Laos during the Vietnam War. He was fun to fly with. (Certainly one simulated forced-landing onto a tiny dirt track was quite interesting!)

As ever, I would test my blood sugar before flying to ensure I wasn't low. I took plenty of carbs with me in the plane, munching away after 30 minutes to avoid going low. Whenever Gillem and I flew together, there was a healthy competitive spirit. Each landing resulted in considerable banter, even after a silky-smooth touchdown. It was great motivation to fly accurately, and Gillem soon flew as if he had several hundred hours under his belt.

Sadly, Ratchaburi Airfield was closed in 1998, one of many casualties of the Thai economic crisis. We switched to the Thai Flying Club (TFC) at Bangphra, a 60-mile drive to the east of Bangkok. TFC nestles between jungle-covered hills, and "base leg" to runway 23 literally brushes by one of these hills before making a sharp left turn onto a short and narrow down-sloping runway. It's a picturesque and exhilarating flying environment.

I flew here regularly with the instructors and Gillem. I often took groups of friends there to fly, but sadly the service was appalling. The flying program was pretty much ignored. People would arrive according to their allotted time and find their plane still out for another hour. It became so frustrating that Gillem stopped flying. I persevered, however, and gradually things improved.

A few months later, I suggested to Gillem that we take two separate aircraft up with instructors and carry out some formation flying. Gillem was curious and agreed. It was great to get him back flying. He only took three flights to "crack" military style formation flying (very close), and we had some immense fun over the following few months. We did high-speed (well, high speed for a Cessna) low passes over Chon Buri Flying Club, a tiny grass strip used for microlights. At Bangphra we would dive down the hill behind runway 23 and speed along 30 feet above the runway in formation. Great fun!

In some countries it was possible to fly gliders and microlights when you have diabetes because of a more relaxed medical system. While Thailand did not have any gliding clubs, there were some active microlight clubs, and in 1999, I joined the Chon Buri Flying Club just a few miles from Bangphra.

Initially I was cynical about microlight flying. The tiny aluminum frames and sail-cloth wings looked fragile. The engine sat directly behind the pilot screaming away at high revs, while a plastic fuel tank sitting right above your head looked like it could spill its flammable load all too easily. Often microlights have airframe parachutes to use in an emergency. However, most of the flying here was between 100–500 feet above ground level, and according to the club, this was insufficient height to open a canopy safely. Hence no parachutes.

Despite the perceived safety issues, I was hooked from the first flight. A good friend Philip and I went up in two separate machines with instructors. When the throttle was opened, the engine behind us screamed, accelerating the machine quickly to lift-off. Two minutes later we were skimming the waters of Lake Bangphra, wind buffeting the body, passengers' legs dangling over the side. It was intoxicating! I had been given the controls from the start, but the instructor hadn't pointed out the air speed indicator perched to one side. I flew in blissful ignorance of our airspeed, even during the approach and landing. When I later discovered my error, I mused that perhaps these machines were safer to fly than I first thought.

The next day I discovered I could get a sport medical and fly solo. *Fantastic.* My Thai girlfriend, Karuna, and I went down to Sri Racha Hospital, and after a quick interview during which I declared my diabetes, I handed over Baht 500 ($12.50) and was the proud owner of a sport medical license. I could now fly solo, albeit in a tiny, fragile, noisy little machine that flew at 30 mph. It was time to have fun on my own.

Every time I flew I would test my blood sugar before takeoff. If I was low, I ate some food and waited until my blood sugar level was at least above 70. However, it was nigh impossible to test while flying in the open air, with 30- or 40-mph winds buffeting your face, body, hands, blood glucose meter and strips. I therefore did my usual thing and munched candy after 30 minutes of being airborne to avoid going low.

The instructors at the microlight club sent me off solo after a couple of hours' practice. This was the first time I'd flown on my own in ten years. I was in heaven, even though I still had some reservations about these tiny, puttering machines. I flew low above Bangphra Lake, circling fishermen in tiny boats and water buffalo, their tails swishing flies off their heads. (There was a very large fly buzzing right overhead.) If a steady southerly breeze blew across the open water, I could fly slowly into wind a few feet above the shoreline, almost hovering in mid-air. Tremendous fun.

A few times I went off around Bangphra Lake for over an hour, just reveling in the freedom. There was a beautiful temple at the far end of the lake, and further along the shoreline, people would look up and wave madly as I buzzed by. On the annual Open Day in 1999, I competed in the "nose-wheel off the ground" competition. On landing I applied a little power and kept the stick aft, thereby keeping the nose-wheel off the ground—until I nearly crashed into a fence at the end of the field. (Yes, I *am* competitive!)

People often ask me whether it's boring to fly a light propeller-driven aircraft compared to flying jets in the RAF. My answer is no. It's flying, and it's immense fun. And you can make it interesting. Sure, I miss the raw power, speed and exhilaration of jet flying, with aerobatics, low-level navigation and formation flying at 500 mph. Even at the age of 41, I am wistful when watching a fast jet flying low over the British countryside. But flying remains a passion.

By 1999 I was flying regularly in both microlights and light aircraft. My skills were getting back up to scratch. But I still didn't have a license for flying general aviation (light) aircraft. *That* was what I really wanted to do. As far as I knew, it was still not possible to do this with diabetes anywhere in the world.

A License Is Possible

One day in 1999 I was flying in a Thai Flying Club Piper Cherokee with Philip in the back seat. As we climbed away from the runway there was a "pop" and a loud whistling noise. The passenger door had just burst open and the instructor sitting on the right was battling to close it again. We leveled off, reduced power and with less propeller slipstream, managed to force the door closed again.

This flight was memorable in more ways than one. The instructor was an American who had validated his U.S. FAA instructor's rating in Thailand, the only non-Thai ever to do this apparently. After learning I had diabetes, he said he thought that America had recently introduced a scheme that could allow me to fly. However, he didn't seem totally convinced. The next week I checked with a locally based FAA designated medical examiner, "Dr. K". Sure enough, I could fly in the U.S. on a full unrestricted private pilot's license (PPL), assuming I could meet the medical requirements. *Wow!* I was amazed, and extremely excited. I desperately wanted to know if I could meet the standards.

Diabetes Control Requirements

Not many people know that it's possible to be a private airplane pilot with insulin-dependent diabetes. A remarkably sensible and effective scheme was introduced in 1997 in the U.S. requiring a pilot to meet the normal requirements of a FAA Class III Medical (for private flying) and also demonstrate that overall diabetes control is good, with no diabetes-related complications.

He or she must have had good diabetes education and developed the ability to self-manage diabetes well.

For good diabetes control, there must be an absence of any recent unexplained hypoglycemic events (i.e. incapacitation) within the last year, and no debilitating diabetes complications, such as damage to the eyes or kidneys or nerves in your legs. Your A1C should reflect good diabetes control as well. Once the medical certificate has been awarded, you must have check-ups every three months and an additional annual medical to confirm continued good diabetes control. These include a report on A1C, daily blood sugar test results, and confirmation of no hypoglycemic events. (Full details of requirements are in Appendix 1.)

When I first applied, the medical reporting requirements seemed daunting. However, Dr. K, the Bangkok-based FAA-designated medical examiner, helped me through what was required. Overall it took seven months to dig out old medical records from the U.K. and supply new reports. Once the regular three-month check-ups were established, I found it an extremely good system. If anything was going wrong with your diabetes control, it would be detected early.

When I sent my medical records and reports to the FAA, I was nervous about the outcome. While I knew that I was well controlled, I didn't want to assume anything. The Medical arrived in the middle of 2000. It was one of the best letters I have ever received.

In-Flight Blood Sugar Control Requirements

So how does the U.S. system ensure safety (primarily avoiding going too low) when flying with diabetes? The FAA sets blood sugar testing requirements: Test within 30 minutes of takeoff, each hour into a flight, and 30 minutes before landing. The results need to fall within a range of 100–300 mg/dl (5.5–16.5 mmol/l). This compares to a non-diabetic range of 72–126 mg/dl and allows a good buffer of safety between 100 and having symptoms of being hypo.

It is a wide, workable range. If the result is above 300, you must land as soon as practicable and bring sugars down into the required range before flying again. (So far I have not gone above 300 when flying.) If your pre-flight test is above 300, you need to administer insulin and/or wait for sugars to fall within range. If a test during flying is below 100, you must ingest 20 g of carbohydrate and bring your sugars back up. (There is no requirement to land if your level is below 100, however.) If testing is difficult to carry out due to flying requirements, such as flying in bad weather, you must eat 20 g carbohydrate and then test when it's convenient. You do not need to send your test results to the FAA after every flight. We are left alone to follow the pre-flight and in-flight testing requirements.

The FAA recently carried out a statistical study of 265 pilots with type 1 diabetes in 1999 and concluded that they were no more likely to suffer an incident or accident with diabetes when flying than any other pilot. After nearly four years of using this system, and flying over 1,200 hours, including a challenging round the world flight, and recently a 12-hour world speed record across the U.S., I find this system both *safe* and *practical*. It is an extremely good way to fly safely with type 1 diabetes.

Testing In Flight

Anyone I've spoken with so far that flies with diabetes seems to develop a technique to minimize the "hands off" time required to test blood sugars. You have to take your hands off the control yoke to insert a test strip into the blood glucose meter, finger-prick for a drop of blood, and then put the drop of blood onto the strip. I carry out each step one at a time, putting my hand back on the controls between each step. The test meter can be attached to a clipboard or the side of the cockpit. You can keep it on your lap, although the higher it is the better it is for peripheral vision to detect movement through the windscreen (if another plane is nearby). Your hand need not come off the controls for more than a few seconds at a time.

What makes testing easier than people may initially think is being able to *trim* the aircraft for straight and level flight. Once trimmed, when you take your hands off the controls, the plane will continue to fly straight and level until turbulence or an aerodynamic imbalance gradually drops a wing and a turn begins. If it's a smooth day, it can be possible to fly straight and level with hands off for half a minute or more. Even in bumpy air, you can often take your hands off the controls for a few seconds and still maintain level flight. Small aircraft can also be steered quite effectively with the rudder pedals if necessary. Pushing the left rudder forward *yaws* the plane to the left, during which the airflow over the left wing slows, generating less lift and resulting in the left wing dropping. The aircraft then turns to the left. While testing, and a wing drops, you can pick it up by pushing the opposite rudder. (Flying hands off is a particularly useful skill to practice in case of a control restriction—one I was thankful for during a real emergency in a single-engine aircraft in 2002.)

I spoke with an Australian Civil Aviation Safety Authority (CASA) medical officer in 2002 who felt that testing in flight was a distraction to flying, and was one reason against flying solo. It is interesting (and to some, extraordinary) that CASA has no requirement for pre-flight or in-flight blood sugar testing. According to the doctor, they would rather have a safety pilot in place who would take control should a severe hypo occur. I think that everyone I have spoken with about this feels the same way: It would be considerably safer to fly solo with frequent blood sugar tests, than to fly accompanied by a safety pilot without testing. There are almost 400 pilots in the U.S., and a few more in Canada and the U.K., who carry out in-flight blood sugar testing. Testing is arguably much less distracting than unraveling a map with both hands during a long cross-country navigation exercise. We could discuss these points for a long time. At the end of the day, the U.S. system demonstrates safe and practical flying with diabetes. Hopefully, in time, other aviation authorities will adopt a similar system.

Two Trips to San Diego

After I received my medical in June 2000, it was time to pay a visit to the U.S. to gain a private pilot license. Although I had been a qualified flying instructor in the Royal Air Force with 530 hours of military flying, I had never obtained a PPL in the U.K. Therefore I couldn't present an existing civilian license to be validated in the U.S. I had to meet a number of flying training requirements and sit a written and practical flying exam.

In October 2000, I took a 16-hour flight from Bangkok to Los Angeles and then drove a rental car 80 miles south to Montgomery Airfield just outside San Diego. The week was busy, flying 12 hours with Aaron, an instructor at American Flyers, to prepare for the test. Although I had been flying Cessna 172s in Thailand, I had to learn various procedures required for U.S. civilian flying. With military flying, we memorized checklists for every action, including pre-takeoff, landing checks and emergency drills. Not so with civilian flying—the instructor and examiner wanted to see you refer to a checklist for every single action.

Aaron was 37 years old and had discovered the joys of flying when he reached his 30s. He had recently resigned from his regular job and was now embarking on a new career in aviation. There is nothing better than an enthusiastic and conscientious instructor, and it was a real pleasure to fly with him. We flew over to Brown Airfield right beside the Mexican border and practiced touch-and-go landings. General handling was to the northeast of San Diego where America's largest avocado-growing region transforms itself into mountainous desert landscape within just 40 miles. It was a fascinating area to fly around. (Tragically, Aaron died in a light aircraft crash in the U.K. the following year.)

I was motivated while at Montgomery Airfield, passing the ground school exam while working hard to prepare for the practical test. It was incredibly frustrating when low cloud and rain blew in from the Pacific for the last two days. The main reason for choosing California was its good weather year round. (I made a mistake. October is approaching the rainy season in Southern California.) The flight test was cancelled, and I returned to Bangkok empty-handed.

Six weeks later I went back, squeezing out my last few days of leave that year. I prepared for two days and then flew the test ride on 5 December 2000. I was nervous. The examiner, JC Boylls, was an extremely jovial man, however, with an amazing knack for making the test flight almost enjoyable. (JC was a very accomplished instructor and examiner, a former winner of an Instructor of the Year award.) It was a hazy day around San Diego, and shortly after takeoff, I was asked to find a tiny mountain airstrip about 15 miles away. By a stroke of luck, I had flown over the same airstrip the day before, and with improved visibility to the east, finding it was relatively straightforward. After the test ride, JC cheerily said, "Congratulations, you are now the newest holder of a private pilot's certificate in the USA" and then stamped *Ace Pilot* in my logbook. It definitely hadn't felt like an ace test ride, but I was elated at passing.

I now had a license! I could fly any aircraft—single engine, twin engine aircraft, even jets—in the U.S. that I wished to be checked out on, solo or with passengers. I could fly at night; I could gain an instrument rating. The opportunities were unlimited. A new chapter of life was about to begin. I flew back to Bangkok feeling on top of the world.

The Freedom to Fly

As soon as I got back to Thailand, I applied to the Thai Department of Aviation to validate my U.S. license. After I sent in the appropriate application forms, Karuna, my girlfriend, who had recently interviewed one of the directors for a television documentary, mentioned my application to him. It's amazing how contacts can help in Thailand, although I will never know if it did help in this case. Two weeks later, I was delighted to receive a Thai flying license.

On March 29, 2001, I took off solo in a Grumman Cheetah and just reveled around the local area, flying steep turns and wingovers. After so many years of flying around Bangphra, it felt amazing to be doing this *ON MY OWN!* I had just been formation flying with Gillem and unbeknownst to me, he was sneakily watching my first solo landing. Even though my dentures remained in place, there was much banter (defamatory abuse!) about heavy landings when we spoke later.

I flew as many times as possible in 2001, sometimes taking the club Cessna 172 or Grumman Cheetah up for three hours at a time. I practiced stalls, steep turns, wingovers and emergency drills galore. I also flew low level around some 2,000-foot jungle-covered mountains nearby. It's a beautiful area with Buddhist temples sitting proudly atop smaller hills. I was catching up on lost time.

Every time I flew I adhered to the U.S. regulations, testing blood sugars 30 minutes before takeoff and ensuring that I was in the 100–300 required range. If I were below 100 before takeoff, I would eat at least 20 g of carbs and retest 20 minutes later, waiting for the results to be above 100 before climbing in and taking off. During each flight, I would place my testing kit on the seat beside me (or in a pocket if a passenger was present) and test each hour into the flight. I was extremely happy to have this flying freedom. I think some of the Thai mechanics thought I was crazy, flying so often and for so long each time. Even Gillem seemed a bit nonplussed at times. I was probably one of the highest-spending club members that year. I flew 150 hours in 2001, not bad considering that work was manic toward the end of that year.

The flying was a great way to relax and refresh myself each week. That was the year I took over as CEO of our Bangkok joint venture, running the company while coordinating the sale of Schroders' stake. At times it was stressful, trying to keep the imminent sale quiet from staff. The Thai marketplace is rife with rumors and soon there were plenty circulating about our company sale. Staff would ask me to clarify the situation. All I could do was confirm that the rumors were indeed rumors. It felt distinctly unpleasant to betray staff loyalty.

In the middle of 2001, I was delighted to discover that Australia had a scheme for people with diabetes to fly on a full license, albeit with a safety pilot. I could validate my U.S. license in Australia, assuming I could pass the Australian regulator's medical requirements. Moreover, Gillem could act as safety pilot when I flew—a great way to share the flying.

In August 2000, Gillem and I traveled to Melbourne and trained for 8 hours each in an old but trusty Piper Aztec, a twin-engine machine. There's nothing better than enjoying great flying experiences with friends. We learned new skills, simulating engine failures, feathering the prop (to keep resistance down), flying and landing with only one engine. We took it in turns to sit in the front, one of us relaxing in the back, monitoring and (predictably) ridiculing each other's flying attempts!

In February 2001, we returned to Melbourne to be signed off on the Aztec. Before going, I contacted the regulator, CASA, and sent all the medical reports required for the Class 2 Medical. I was impressed that the medical team processed my medical within a week, knowing that I was coming down to Australia from Bangkok.

We were checked out on Papa Alpha Charlie, a 30-plus-year-old Aztec. We now had validated licenses, and I now had my CASA medical. The next day we set off on an ambitious flight on our own from Melbourne to Tasmania. Gillem flew the first leg, passing over the Tasman Sea to land at Devenport on the north coast of Tasmania. It was a stunningly clear day with 100-mile visibility to tree-clad mountains rising high above the forested landscape, a view likely unchanged for millions of years.

I flew the second leg from Devenport back to Melbourne via sparsely populated Flinders Islands. Boy, it was remote down there. Twice that day we were far enough out to sea that no land was in sight, and it was a bit disconcerting flying over cold, remote Tasman Sea waters, home of Great White sharks. Not long after we reached the mainland, we listened to a female Air Traffic Controller talking with an aircraft somewhere in the outback. She seemed to be having a problem with his position and time reports and was giving him a hard time. He was getting quite frustrated. Radio silence. Then, suddenly out of the blue came a new voice: "I reckon she doesn't get out much. Do ya luv?" It took some time to stop laughing.

Two months later, in April 2001, Gillem and three friends, Hugh, Noirin and Liz, and I went back to Melbourne and spent six glorious days flying around Australia. We covered 2,900 miles from Melbourne to Ayres Rock, Alice Springs, Broken Hill—a whirlwind tour in stunning autumn conditions. Visibility was well over 100 miles over Simpson Desert sand dunes and the beautiful Flinders Ranges near Alice Springs. We flew low over Lake Frome and Lake Eyre and dropped into tiny settlements with just a handful of hardy inhabitants.

After three days we were trying to find the remotest possible dirt strips, adding to the spirit of adventure. On booking the hotel at Innaminka by telephone, I asked how we could get from the dirt strip to the hotel, about a mile away. The owner drawled, "Just fly over the roof, we'll hear you and drive out." Slightly bemused by this response I asked "How low over the roof?" He replied "Just as long as you don't take the aerial off the roof, that's fine!"

Throughout our Australian flying, I used the U.S. blood testing requirements. It struck me as a much safer way to operate than Australia's "safety pilot no testing required" system. We were flying for three hours at a time, and I wanted to know where my sugars were. If I went hypo, it could put Gillem as safety pilot, plus my three passengers, into a potentially dangerous situation. Indeed, the Aztec had an autopilot, so I was flying hands off most of the time and testing was extremely straightforward. I made sure my diabetes kit bag was available in the cockpit with blood glucose meter, insulin and syringe, plus plenty of carbohydrates. Throughout the cross-country adventure, I was able to keep my sugars within the U.S. FAA range of 100–300.

I couldn't have been happier flying a twin engine plane around Australia and over some of the most arid, remote parts of the world. It was food for thought that soon turned into a meal.

Chapter:

6 Dare to Dream

Man who say it cannot be done should not interrupt man doing it.

—Old Chinese proverb

A New Dream

For years I had been fascinated by stories of people flying in remote areas. I enjoyed reading *Fate is the Hunter* by Ernest Gann, a riveting story of pioneering piston engine flights over the North Atlantic and other parts of the world. I was intrigued by solo round-the-world flights in tiny aircraft. *Flight of the Kiwi* was a story of undaunted courage from Cliff Tait flying around the world in a tiny under-powered single-engine plane from New Zealand. His flights over the inhospitable North Atlantic, Arab deserts and stormy Asian tropical waters were captivating. Such an adventure appealed enormously to me. In 1999, when I discovered that it was possible to fly with a license, I suddenly thought, *Why not do the same yourself? And while doing it, raise awareness of diabetes and funds for diabetes research.*

No! Would I really dare to do this? It seemed like a mad idea at the time. How could I afford such a dream project? And when would I ever get the time? It would take months to plan such a flight, and months to complete. The amount of preparations would be vast. I would have to gain an instrument rating, radio licenses, and official permission to fly over the Middle

East, Asia and the Pacific and learn about international flying procedures. There were so many unknowns. I put the idea to the back of my mind. However, I quietly resolved to save money over the following years, just in case an opportunity arose.

The Opportunity

In early 2002 my parent employer, Schroders, sold its Thai joint venture, and my work contract finished. Suddenly I had an opportunity to carry out a world flight. I was fired up. I worked out a detailed business plan on my computer and worked out that I'd saved just enough to finance the project myself. However, I did not want to tell anyone except Karuna and my family in case the sale of the joint venture deal did not go through. I also told Tom Claytor who was based in Thailand and had been carrying out a lifetime project of flying around the world in his Cessna 180 single-engine airplane. Tom's story and activities had helped inspire my plan, and I was delighted that he was willing to act as an advisor. However, he told a few other people. Gillem's initial response to Tom (who was highlighting some of the difficult organizational challenges) was, "He'll never do it!" Tom thought that it would be great to prove my old friend wrong. But this was not an issue. I wanted to do this flight for myself and for diabetes. (It must be noted that Gillem's initial response of healthy cynicism rapidly changed to one of encouragement and support.)

Tom proved to be an invaluable advisor, and while brainstorming one day, we came up with the name Diabetes World Flight (DWF). He was tremendously enthusiastic, but also cynical at first. "Are you *really* going to do it?" he asked on a few occasions. Tom had already flown his single-engine Cessna 180 over the North Atlantic and Arctic regions, Europe, Africa and the Middle East before reaching Thailand. He knew the enormous undertaking of a round-the-world flight, the challenges and frustrations that I would encounter.

I, too, was aware of the enormous challenge, and yes, I did have several apprehensions. I would be taking a risk with personal safety. I had been in paid employment since 1984 and would have to take at least 15 months off from the finance industry, without any security. I would chew up a large proportion of my savings. That's enough to make any Scotsman quake in his boots.

Aims

There were important messages I wanted to spread by carrying out a world flight with diabetes. I wanted to demonstrate to aviation authorities around the world that flying was safe according to U.S. flying regulations. I also wanted to demonstrate and emphasize that diabetes need not limit the scope of peoples' dreams and ambitions.

I also wanted to raise funds for diabetes research. The stated mission behind DWF was: To be the first licensed pilot with type 1 diabetes to fly around the world and raise funds for diabetes research. In March 2002, I established a project website (www.diabetesworldflight.com) with the able assistance of Lisa Frost, the "web mistress" in Thailand and later in Singapore. The British diabetes association, Diabetes UK, agreed to collect donations via a credit card payment page facility on my website. The plan was to contact diabetes-related companies, friends and others to make donations while I flew the world flight.

Funding

When I first struck on the idea of carrying out a world flight in 1999, having a few months' spare time, buying a plane and financing a world flight seemed out of the question. I estimated that the operating costs of flying a twin with a safety pilot would be up to $100,000. I could budget up to $130,000 to buy a plane, and another $50,000 to cover five months of expenses while preparing for a twin rating (license) and instrument rating, building flying hours, living in the U.S., insuring the plane, plus incidentals and a contingency fund for things that could go wrong. The total cash outlay would be $280,000 U.S., a huge amount for me to cover. However, I had saved enough over the previous three years that if the plane could be sold afterward, I could *just* afford it. I was extremely grateful to have this flexibility.

At the same time, I was very keen to gain sponsorship. Not long after departing for the U.S. in April, Tom Claytor sent an email saying, "Surround yourself with those who support you." It was a tremendous piece of advice. Eluned, a great old friend in London, worked in corporate marketing and sponsorship, and she took on the challenge with me. Between the two of us, we drafted a detailed sponsorship proposal. Of any corporate sponsorship gained, I would allocate 40% to cover operating costs while 60% would be donated to diabetes research. Individuals' donations would go 100% to research. By the time I started DWF, however, I decided to allocate 100% of all donated funds directly to diabetes research.

I soon found out just how challenging sponsorship hunts were. Marketing officers are busy people and receive countless sponsorship requests. Teams have to be convinced. Funding needs to be available. Any proposal would need to stand out—the more professionally packaged the better. I sent a basic sponsorship proposal to several large diabetes and aviation-related companies. None of these were acknowledged. I spent many hours with follow-up telephone calls. Persistence can pay, but rebuttals prevailed.

The economic situation in the U.K. and U.S. after the 9/11 World Trade Center terrorist attack was difficult. I was applying four months into a new financial year and after marketing plans had already been decided. However, one approach met with some encouraging feedback. The Accu-Check blood glucose meter office in the U.K. referred me to their PR agency, Edelman, in London. In March 2002, I met Zahir White who seemed very enthusiastic. He promised to send a proposal to Accu-Chek's parent company, Roche. However, nothing came back over the next few months despite several follow-up calls.

Three weeks before DWF departure, the Edelman London office suggested contacting their Chicago office, just 400 miles from Omaha where I was based in the U.S. The following week I met with the Edelman healthcare team, and they loved the idea. A few days later, Peter Sebastian at Accu-Chek Global Marketing agreed to supply blood glucose meters and test strips, arrange media coverage for the first flight and make a donation to research of $1,000. Initially I was quite taken aback at how little the donation was, particularly given how large the company was, and the huge amount of time, effort and money I had invested in Diabetes World Flight. (It's easy to become emotional about your own project; I was guilty of this.) However, this was a non-budgetary item for Accu-Chek. I was grateful for their support. It was a loose arrangement—no formal agreement was made—but I could discuss similar media and donation possibilities with Edelman in other countries. (In total Accu-Chek donated more than $10,000 for activities in the U.S., U.K., Singapore and Australia.)

Little did I know that my contact with Edelman would lead to one of the most unbelievable coincidences of my life. Unbeknownst to me, my ex-wife, Chrissy, had joined Edelman in Singapore and was working on the local

Accu-Chek account. Three months later at a press conference, we would meet for the first time in almost nine years.

There were several other sponsors. I was extremely grateful to gain support from Air BP. This arose after an enjoyable dinner with general aviation enthusiasts in Dubai. One dinner guest, Evelyn Brey, rang Giri, the Air BP regional manager, and asked if Air BP could support DWF. Giri became an instant supporter and offered to fill up my gas tanks at eight airports (with Air BP gas) from Dubai and Australia.

Another stroke of good fortune came through a friend of a friend, Michelle, working extremely hard behind the scenes to gain general sponsorship. She contacted U.S. multinationals on my behalf, got her brother to draft press releases, and ended up arranging excellent support from Sheraton Hotels in Bahrain, Oman and Mumbai. I was extremely impressed by Michelle's dedication and very grateful for her support.

There were several other pleasant surprises on the way around the world. Eurocontrol, responsible for charging fees on aircraft flying on instrument flight plans through Europe, waived navigation fees, saving me several hundred dollars. Greer Aviation Ltd., the fixed base operator (FBO) at Prestwick Airport in Scotland, waived a landing fee. Jeppessen sponsored all the maps and charts for the North Atlantic crossing. This was worth a few hundred dollars. In Thailand, Bill Heinecke of Minor International Group kindly arranged sponsored accommodation at the Bangkok Marriott Resort and Spa and the JW Marriott Phuket Resort and Spa Hotel. A couple of Australian airports waived their fees (although I kept receiving bills through the post for a few months afterward!). And after I finished the flight, Global Aerospace, that had underwritten the worldwide insurance for the plane, reimbursed half of the $3,250 premium to be donated to the research fundraising. I remain very grateful to all the people and companies that supported DWF.

Chapter:

7 Preparations

Some people regard discipline as a chore. For me, it is a kind of order that sets me free to fly.
— Julie Andrews, legendary singer and actress

You win not by chance but by preparation.
— Roger Maris, legendary baseball player

A Hefty Task List

In total it took five and a half months to complete preparations. It soon seemed like I was working a full-time job again with plenty of overtime and stress to boot.

First of all, I had to relocate to the U.S., where my flying license was domiciled. I then had to go through a long and detailed task list. I had to get an instrument rating and twin rating to fly the type of plane I had in mind. I had to find and purchase a second-hand aircraft, arrange insurance, install auxiliary fuel tanks (for over-water flights as long as 2,000 miles) and a long-range HF radio (like a ham radio) for long-distance communication during oceanic flights. I needed to get a radio license for the plane and myself. To learn international radio procedures. To plan the exact route, arrange maps and charts for each flight and organize survival equipment required by Canadian regulations for the inhospitable North Atlantic crossing. To arrange navigation databases for GPS navigation systems, find a clearance agent to gain permission to fly into nine countries and overhead five countries in the Middle East, Asia and the Pacific Ocean. To make sure I had accepted credit cards to pay for fuel and navigation charges, or sufficient cash with me. I needed to find a webmaster and establish a website with a facility allowing donations to be made to diabetes research. I needed to design a DWF logo and business cards. I wanted to find potential sponsors from the diabetes industry. I also needed to contact diabetes associations in each country I would visit.

Toward the end of 2001 while still working, I spent many spare-time hours poring over an atlas and websites to decide the best route. I read an aircraft reference book to select a potential twin-engine aircraft. When I stopped working in January 2002, I had already decided the route and suitable aircraft models to look for.

Some people asked me why I based myself out of the U.S. This was easy to answer. I had a pilot's license in the U.S., the only country that offered me full freedom to fly with diabetes. As long as I was flying a U.S.-registered plane with a U.S. license and medical, this would make entry into foreign countries legal, assuming any other permission requirements were met. When I traveled to the U.S. in April 2002, however, I had no idea where I would live. It would most likely be where I found the aircraft, and the world flight would begin from there.

One major task to complete was finding a safety pilot to accompany me outside the U.S., as my Class III medical certificate has a very clear statement printed on the front, *Not valid outside the borders of the U.S.* Basically I needed someone who would be qualified and insured to fly my plane. Technically I would be using the safety pilot's license and medical certificate to allow me to act as Pilot in Command (PIC).

The safety pilot would have to be happy sitting in the co-pilot's seat and doing nothing for four months or more. (A tall order. It's not easy for a pilot to sit in a cockpit and do nothing for a long period of time.) I was determined to carry out the whole flight as if it were solo, i.e., as if I were on my own. This was an extremely important aspect of Diabetes World Flight. If the flight were carried out with two pilots helping each other, the message about flying safely with type 1 diabetes would have been weakened.

I drafted a written agreement with the safety pilot that made these points clear, and that he or she was there for legal purposes only. The only time intervention would be necessary was if I was about to *bust* airspace (fly illegally) or be incapacitated if my blood sugar was too low. I outlined that the latter should be avoided due to the in-flight blood sugar test requirements.

Flying Training

When I set out for the U.S. in April 2002, I had much flying training to do before starting DWF. I needed to gain a twin-engine aircraft rating and an instrument rating in the U.S. (required for solo international flights). I also wanted to build at least 150 hours of flying time, thereby increasing my overall experience and, hopefully, making insurance easier to arrange.

In early April I took a British Airways flight from London to Miami. One of life's coincidences happened while waiting in the Miami passport control line. Al Matthews, a pilot I knew from RAF days, was waiting in the crew line in his BA pilot's uniform. He had been flying my commercial flight over from London. We enjoyed a quick chat and mused over how small the world is.

I then spent 10 days at Fort Lauderdale Executive Airport where I flew 13 hours of training with Ty Semons, a quiet and conscientious instructor. I already had a twin rating in Australia but still had to pass the FAA system. The U.S. required a formal practical and oral exam, while in Australia it was a short written test, and then the instructor signed you off once you were deemed competent to fly the designated twin-engine machine.

It was good to consolidate twin handling and theory in the U.S. Ty remarked that I was one of his harder-working students. He had no idea that I was on a mission. I hadn't told him in case I failed the U.S. twin rating. I was also extremely keen to improve knowledge of twin-aircraft systems before starting DWF.

We had some interesting experiences in the first week. The flying school's Piper Seneca I twin was a pig to land. Her controls were unresponsive at slow speed, and extremely heavy on final approach, requiring so much rearward trim that I had to *push forward* on the control wheel just before landing. Not good. After three nail-biting days, I switched to an old Piper Aztec. It was more expensive to fly but at least I knew the Aztec controls were light and more responsive. It felt *safer*. However, this old Aztec had seen better days. Not long after the first takeoff, the front door burst open with a deafening roar. Ty struggled to close it and eventually succeeded. Our climb rate was anemic, and it took some head scratching and experimenting with the fuel mixture controls to rectify the problem.

On the second Aztec day, I flew a memorable cross-country flight to the Florida Keys. On the way back we flew 30 feet above the waves, at one stage catching a fleeting glimpse of a surfacing turtle. Stunning stuff! However, at the end of this heart-thumping trip, there was a long list of *squawks*—items to be fixed. The Aztec seemed to be falling apart. There was no choice, I had to brave the Seneca once again.

I worked solidly for the next few days to prepare for the oral and practical exam. We flew to the east of Fort Lauderdale, practicing general handling, stalls, steep turns, minimum control speed demonstrations, simulated engine failures and single-engine landings. It was hard physical work at the Seneca's heavy controls. Engine out procedures require heavy rudder pressure to counteract asymmetric power. I was amazed to find I had lost four pounds by the end of the 10 days' training.

The hard work paid off. The check ride went fine, and my landing was the best yet (still a solid "cruncher" mind you). The examiner congratulated me with some gusto. He also found this particular Seneca a pig to land.

Alligator Food

After adding twins to the U.S. license in April, I based myself temporarily at Fort Pierce further up the Florida coast where I also looked at an old 1969 Beech Baron B55. At Fort Pierce airfield, I was checked out on a flight school Cessna 172 and flew this for a couple of hours each day for a week.

The U.S. flying system has tremendous rules for low flying. Over uninhabited land, you can go as low as you like (dare) ensuring 500 feet clearance from people or man-made structures. In most other countries, you have to maintain a minimum of 500 feet above ground, regardless of how remote or uninhabited.

I find low-level flying extremely exhilarating, although it's best tempered with some caution. The Fort Pierce Airfield is based near Lake Okeechobee, a huge reservoir to the west. In between there are alligator-infested swamps and Cyprus Pine Lake, named after the trees that ring the shoreline. I flew along swamps at 20 feet, around clumps of trees and the shoreline of Cyprus

Pine Lake. One afternoon I spied an alligator head just above the lake's surface. Pulling up sharply I could see the whole alligator's body submerged in the water—it was *huge*. I wondered if he (or she) was waiting for this rather annoying metallic fly buzzing overhead to drop in and offer dinner. I exercised some caution in this man-eating environment, flying close enough to Cyprus Pine Lake shoreline that if the engine failed I could pull up, clear the trees and land on the other side in open fields. I simulated this emergency a number of times to make sure it would work; I really didn't fancy being alligator food.

I also flew near the shoreline of Lake Okeechobee, just feet above the water. Whenever a water surface is smooth and calm, however, it can be perilously difficult to gauge one's height. If a wave is just 2 inches high but you judge it to be 2 feet, you are *extremely* close to the water. If you fly into blinding evening sunshine, it's even worse. Ideally you need at least small waves and/or a shoreline to gauge height more accurately and safely. Another danger is birds at low level. Keeping a good lookout is required, and you need to be prepared for avoiding action. Over the week at Fort Pierce I flew 10 hours in six days. The more I flew, the more I *wanted* to fly. I was extremely happy. However, I still needed to find a plane.

Move to the Midwest

After a week, I moved on to New Jersey to look at a Cessna 310R twin and then on to Omaha, Nebraska, to look at a Baron E55. The day after arriving in Omaha, I crossed the Missouri River into Iowa to fly at Council Bluffs Airfield. This small airfield lies atop rolling hills and is surrounded by cornfields. It's a peaceful and attractive spot. The people at Advanced Air Inc., the FBO, were helpful and friendly. I liked it a lot.

That night I went night flying with Chris, a young and diligent instructor, and was checked out on a Cessna 172. There was a good practice area to the east, while 1,200 feet above the airfield and to the west lay Omaha "Class C" controlled airspace. I thought it was a great spot, and it would be good practice to operate near and around controlled airspace. I decided to base myself at Council Bluffs and train for the instrument rating (IR).

I had been concerned about the IR. It would be hard work to cover all the theory and practical procedures. Single-pilot instrument flying requires

100% absolute concentration, solid radio communication, spatial awareness and exacting procedural skills. Tom Claytor suggested not bothering with the rating and relying on the safety pilot's instrument rating instead. However, the aim behind DWF was to carry it out *as if it were solo.* An instrument rating was required for international legs. I was determined to get it.

I was assigned to Brian Enenbach, a 26-year-old instructor. He seemed quiet for the first few flights but was meticulous, having notched up a 100% pass rate with his students. He could answer just about any question I asked him, and if he didn't know, we looked up the answer in the relevant manual. An excellent student/instructor relationship developed (it didn't take Brian long to mimic the good old British exclamation, "Bloody Hell!").

I studied hard for the IR over three weeks, passing the written test while flying 27 training hours in total. Then on June 25th I passed the instrument-rating exam in Sioux City, 80 miles north of Council Bluffs. As I flew back to Council Bluffs, I felt an enormous pressure had lifted from my shoulders. I could now focus on finding a plane and completing the world flight preparations.

The Plane

When I was making the initial plans, I considered using a single-engine aircraft, but ultimately I chose a twin-engine aircraft because of the safety of having two engines for flights over vast tracts of ocean water. If one engine failed at cruise altitude, I should have been able to turn around or continue to my destination on the remaining engine, just at slower speed. A larger, faster machine appealed greatly. It was more akin to commercial flying, possibly adding more weight to the argument for safe flying with diabetes.

Safety in twins is a debatable issue, however. Some pilots argue that after suffering engine failure in a twin, the remaining one just "takes you to the scene of disaster more quickly." Indeed, if an engine fails when the plane is heavy and slow, the asymmetric power (of the good engine perched out to one side on the wing) will result in a strong yaw and roll toward the failed engine. If close to the ground and not handled deftly, the aircraft can spiral into the ground. You need to determine quickly and *correctly* which engine has failed and then take action. *Fly the plane*—then *throttle, mixture, propeller pitch levers all forward, gear up and flaps up (to reduce drag), dead leg = dead engine (the leg with no rudder pressure), confirm (by closing dead engine throttle). Once confirmed dead, if soon after takeoff and close to the ground, feather the dead engine's prop to reduce drag and position to land.*

If a single-engine plane loses power, your options are very straightforward. *Lower the nose, establish a safe gliding speed and attempt to make a safe landing on the ground or water ahead. If time permits, try to restart the engine.* There is no asymmetric power to handle. The arguments for each side of the debate are strong. I felt comfortable flying a twin. However, I was aware of the dangers. If an engine failed, I really needed to be on the ball.

Eventually I decided on a Beech Baron, with its reputation for solid build and an efficient cruise of around 200 mph. Most importantly, it had one of the best single engine climb rates of any twin, at around 380 feet per minute. In case of an engine failure, this would help the aircraft remain aloft when it was overweight with extra gas during the world flight. I also confess to liking the Baron's looks—she's a good looker.

I knew I was wet behind the ears when it came to buying a plane, and I really didn't want to buy a lemon. I had been warned to be careful and cynical. I heeded the advice.

Although there are hundreds of aircraft in the second-hand aircraft market, I had specific criteria to meet that made the hunt more challenging. The criteria included de-icing equipment, weather radar, GPS navigation equipment, and mid-time engines that would normally be well worn-in (halfway between the 1,700-hour time needed for a full overhaul). I also needed to sell the aircraft soon after finishing, so I wanted a plane with little or no damage history. This lengthy list of requirements led to a wild goose chase around America, taking four months to complete. The hunt started in Florida and took me to New Jersey, Nebraska, Oklahoma and Minnesota.

In June I offered $150,000 for a 1973 model Beech Baron E55 in the Midwest. It was more expensive than I had budgeted but had everything I needed including a state-of-the-art Garmin GPS navigation system. After accepting the offer, however, the owner seemed to behave oddly. Initially he refused to agree to my chosen maintenance company to carry out a pre-purchase inspection. It seemed as if he was scared that the pre-purchase inspection would find something wrong with the plane, leading to expensive repairs before the sale. My alarm bells rang loudly. Fortunately the decision was taken out of my hands. A week later the owner explained that his plane had failed an expensive propeller airworthiness directive. There was no cost-effective or speedy solution. I had to look for another aircraft.

I was beginning to think that the plane purchase was jinxed. It was now early July, and I was supposed to be starting the trip at the end of August. I was frustrated and furious. This particular incident had wasted precious time, money and effort. I really was back to square one and running out of time. I launched another internet search, and widened the net to include slightly larger Baron B58s. I found an excellent prospect in Rochester, Minnesota, a 1970 Beech Baron B58, with high airframe time but mid-time engines. It had extended range fuel tanks giving six hour's endurance, and it was cheap, being sold by a new FBO owner who had no use for it. I rang the seller, and we agreed to a viewing. However, when I rang back two hours later with follow-up questions, the B58 had just been sold. *Damn!* Back to square one again.

I contacted two more sellers. One was Jim Hanson, the owner of Albert Lea FBO in Minnesota, who had a B58 and an older C55 for sale. The B58 was a 1970 vintage and had longer-range tanks. This sounded good. He flew it down to Council Bluffs Airport, and we test-flew it together. (He didn't like my steep wingovers, his hands twitching toward the controls!) I reviewed the logbooks in detail. There was something familiar about this plane. Indeed, it was the same B58 that I had agreed to look at the previous week.

No doubt Jim had bought the B58 at a knockdown price and was going to make a decent return on his investment. I really needed this plane. Jim was a seasoned bargainer, and we eventually agreed on $138,200. The pre-purchase inspection took 10 days to complete and only a few minor squawks were found that needed repairing. I was immensely relieved that it was in sound shape. I finally had my airplane.

Before I could buy N30TB, I had to establish a trust company to own the aircraft, as non-U.S. citizens are not allowed to own U.S. aircraft directly. It cost $2,000 to establish the trust and another $900 for a year's administration fee. The funds were duly transferred, the sale completed. Finally insurance was arranged, and on August 2, 2002, I took possession of N30TB (November Three Zero Tango Bravo). I was the proud owner of a twin-engine, beautiful Beech Baron B58.

Challenges

Organizational challenges come with the territory of a project like Diabetes World Flight. For me, three tasks proved particularly challenging—arranging aircraft insurance, finding a company to install auxiliary tanks and securing a safety pilot.

Although I was 39 years old and had 870 hours flying time in April 2002, with 400 hours on military jets and 87 on twins, I was considered inexperienced by the companies who might insure a world flight in a twin. In April I got a ball-park quote of "up to $20,000" for a Baron B55 worth $120,000. This seemed ridiculously expensive, but the World Trade Center terrorist attack had resulted in heavy insurance losses worldwide, and insurers were now more risk averse and needed to recoup losses. I had budgeted for $12,000 at most for insurance. I had no choice. I would have to bear this cost, even if it broke my $100,000 operating cost budget.

When I requested a formal quote for a Baron in May, I was devastated to be told that no U.S. firm was willing to underwrite the risk for a world flight. No specific reason was given. At that time there were tensions between nuclear powers India and Pakistan. Middle East tensions were also increasing over Iraq. My relative inexperience would have been the main reason.

Earlier in the year, I had considered not insuring the plane. Maybe if I ditched and survived, perhaps I could sell the story and recoup my losses. However, I discovered that liability insurance was mandatory for international flights, as was rescue insurance in the North Atlantic. I had to find another way. I briefly checked into Australian insurance (of an Australian registered plane) and yes, it was possible. Not only that, it was cost effective. The Australian dollar was extremely weak and aircraft were therefore 30% cheaper to buy in U.S. dollar terms. If I based myself out of Australia, after finishing DWF, I could ferry the plane over the Pacific and sell it for a profit in the U.S.

However, there was one major drawback to flying in Australia. I could not fly solo and therefore could not build time or train without the hassle of finding a safety pilot *every* time I flew. The United States, however, offered total freedom for its pilots with diabetes. I decided to stick with America. The message behind flying safely with diabetes would be much stronger.

In March I visited Bruno Schroder, the family representative at Schroders, my old employer. Bruno Schroder owned a smart Pilatus PC-12 turboprop and had flown his own world flight a few years earlier. He is passionate about flying, and during our meeting, he went through a checklist of items that I would need to complete. His secretary entered the room twice to remind him of imminent meetings, but he cancelled them both—he was enjoying the fly-talk.

I am very grateful indeed to Bruno Schroder for referring me to Simon Macfadyen, an enthusiastic and likeable character who worked with Marsh Specialties Limited in London. Simon loved the idea of Diabetes World Flight and spoke with Philip Gregory of Global Aerospace U.K. who also liked the idea. Literally the day after I received the devastating news about no U.S. insurer being willing to cover the flight, Simon gave me verbal confirmation over the telephone. "Yes!" Not only was coverage possible, the quote was less than half the original quote in the U.S. It would cost $9,250 in total, $6,000 for U.S. coverage, and $3,250 for international coverage for the world flight—well within budget. I was enormously relieved. DWF could now go ahead as planned.

However, there were a couple of other challenges to overcome yet. Beech Barons normally have sufficient fuel for up to 1,000 miles range if cruising at economy power settings. The longest leg between Hawaii and San Francisco would be 2026 nautical miles (2,329 land miles). Therefore, I needed to install auxiliary fuel tanks, or ferry tanks, in the main cabin to extend range to around 2,500 miles.

At the beginning of the year, Tom had referred me to a company he was familiar with in the U.S. However this company was suffering from recently imposed regulations for installing ferry tanks. This came about after a Twin Comanche suffered engine failure shortly after takeoff while flying over the North Atlantic. The overweight, under-powered Twin Comanche made a good belly landing, but during deceleration the tanks shifted forward and crushed the pilot to death. Not only was this a disturbing revelation, but more challenging installation requirements for ferry tanks had been imposed. The company could not install tanks on a Baron for the foreseeable future.

I was in Thailand for a 10-day break when I discovered this and subsequently spent the next two days searching on the internet and making countless U.S. telephone calls to try to find an alternative company. I was bounced from one company to the next. Nobody would install ferry tanks for an independent pilot due to liability issues. At 3 a.m. on the second night, I was referred to Ed Therrien of Aircraft International Services at Hayward Executive Airport near San Francisco. Ed seemed very relaxed. It would be "no problem" to install tanks for a Baron. "Just give a couple of week's notice when the time comes." The four back seats would be taken out and two individual 110-gallon aluminum tanks squeezed in. These would allow 15 hours endurance or 2,500 nautical miles for a standard Baron B55. Fuel flow could be switched from the main tanks (in the wings) to the ferry tanks using four levers positioned on the floor-well immediately behind the co-pilot's seat. The cost was $2,500, roughly what I had estimated. *Great!* At 3:30 a.m. I fell into a deep and relieved sleep.

The last challenge was a sticky one. Imagine being asked a question, "How would you like to spend four months flying around the world, visiting fascinating countries and tropical islands, and be paid for it?" Sounds tempting? I suspect so. However, it was very difficult to find a safety pilot with the right experience, age *and* the available time. A married person was unlikely to leave a family for so long. There were plenty of young, single pilots who were keen, but the insurance underwriter refused coverage for lack of flying experience and youth.

The safety pilot also had to feel happy to sit in the cockpit and do nothing for four months or more. The plan was to carry out DWF as if it were a solo flight. Ask any pilot what it's like to sit in a cockpit and do nothing for long periods of time. It's extremely difficult. You want to pass commentary, make suggestions, and your hands will likely twitch for the controls every now and then.

Two weeks after stopping work, I contacted JC Boylls, my examiner in San Diego, who referred me to James Aiden, a British instructor with U.S. ratings. This worked perfectly. I met James at White Waltham Airfield in March and liked him immediately. He was 44 and had U.S. instructor ratings. His dad had type 2 diabetes, hence he loved the idea behind DWF. He seemed highly spirited and very professional toward his flying and had already made three ferry flights across the North Atlantic in light aircraft. This would help insurance coverage. I offered James the job. "I'd love to visit all those exotic places!" he replied, and accepted. *Wow!* By March I had a safety pilot already. It seemed too good to be true.

It *was* too good to be true. A few weeks later James contacted me to say he could only fly the North Atlantic crossing to the U.K. I offered Brian, my Omaha-based instructor, the position from the U.K. onward. He was keen. With his 26 years and 2,500 hours flying experience, 300 of which were on twins, the insurance company accepted him. However, in July Brian received a great offer from ACA, a regional airline. Understandably, he accepted the job. (I would have done the same—much better sitting in a Regional Jet cockpit than a cramped Baron cockpit with a crusty old Scotsman.)

The search began again. It was getting close to departure time, and I was beginning to worry. I found a tall 38-year-old instructor at Millard Airfield in Omaha. He loved the idea but was less than enthusiastic about sitting and doing nothing in the cockpit. A week later he informed me that he'd gained a charter flying job and that he couldn't come.

It was now late August, less than four weeks to departure. I asked Chris, the 23-year-old instructor based at Council Bluffs. Like Brian, he was keen (his mom wasn't!). However, the insurance company refused coverage on the basis of too few hours and age. I was now getting desperate. Without another safety pilot, I couldn't go any further than the U.K.

As a last ditch chance, I contacted Ty Semons, the instructor I'd trained with in Florida in April. I had asked Ty in April, but he had replied no, citing that the timing would clash with his application for a government service job. After two days of nail biting, I saw an email reply from Ty. Anxiously, I opened it. He had been thinking hard and after discussing it with his fiancée, Maria, he had decided to accept the offer. The government service dates were unlikely to clash after all. He could quit his instructing job at Fort Lauderdale Executive Airport whenever I needed him. Ty was 37 years old and had logged 3,000 hours flying, and although only 100 were on twins, the insurance company accepted him. *FANTASTIC!* All he had to do was fly five hours with Brian for familiarization. It was an *immense* relief. At long last I had the second safety pilot.

The following weekend, Ty flew up from Miami and flew his required five hours in N30TB with Brian. While having a drink in downtown Omaha, Ty quietly mentioned how Maria had been instrumental in his decision to come along. She had thought it would be good for him. I was extremely grateful to them both.

Stress and Diabetes Control

I was asked whether some of the organizational stress of Diabetes World Flight pushed my blood sugars up from time to time. The answer is yes. However, frequent blood sugar testing detected these highs, at which point I injected short-acting insulin. If time permitted, 30 minutes later (once it had begun to work in the system) I would go for a jog or a swim to bring sugars down more quickly. I remember swimming in the middle of the night a few times in 2002 to try to get my blood sugar back down to normal levels. Despite the occasional highs, in the first half of 2002, my A1Cs were in the low 6% range, so fortunately the short-term stress did not seem to affect my average blood sugar control. (I have seen suggestions that short bursts of high blood sugars do not cause significant damage to internal organs. However, I don't want to take any chances—I still try to keep any high periods as short as possible.)

Suspected Terrorist

Early in 2002 I wondered if anyone might find my activities suspicious. I was a foreigner, albeit British, flying a plane around the U.S. less than a year after 9/11. Installing auxiliary gas tanks would render flying quite thought provoking—an extra 220 gallons of flammable gas would slosh around right behind me. (In my own thoughts, I recalled an old pilots' saying, "The only time an aircraft has too much fuel on board is when it is on fire.")

Shortly after arriving in Omaha, I used the Carter Lake Public Library. The three librarians, Mary, Theresa and Shawnee noticed that I was using the library internet to look at photographs of aircraft (for sale). They remembered that 9/11 terrorists had used public library internet stations to communicate and wondered if my activities could be suspicious. They were joking— a little. There was a serious undertone to their discussions. A few days later, I chatted with Mary and gave her my card highlighting Diabetes World Flight. They were amused but also relieved to find out what I was up to.

More than three months later, I landed N30TB late on a Friday night at Council Bluffs Airport. As I drove into Omaha, it was dark, and I was thinking about the flight I'd just done. A blue light suddenly flashed at the side of the road. I looked at my speedometer. It was almost 50 mph in a 35-mph zone. *Damn!*

I pulled over and a police officer came up to the door, asking for ID. Detecting my foreign accent, he asked me what I was doing in Council Bluffs. I handed him my Diabetes World Flight business card, explaining that I was a British citizen and flying my plane out of Council Bluffs as part of a world flight project. I then handed over my Thai driver's license and car insurance documents.

I can imagine his alarm bells going off. I was a British national with a Thai driver's license, driving a beaten up old car and flying a plane out of Council Bluffs. *Hmmm!* As the officer handed me a written warning for speeding, he said, "You can do what you like with this. Burn it, throw it away or frame it." He then asked me what room I was in at the local Super 8 Motel. I didn't think anything of this question. I was just relieved to drive away without being fined.

Three days afterward, late on Monday morning, I checked out of the Super 8 Motel to take the Baron to San Francisco. Just 20 minutes later, three men from the Immigration & Naturalization Service (INS) burst through the motel entrance, raced upstairs and apparently almost beat my door down. No answer. They returned to the ground floor and asked the receptionist, Dianne, "Where is Mr. Cairns? We have reason to believe that he is a suspected terrorist."

Dianne was incredulous and laughed out loud, "What! You must be joking! Douglas! A terrorist? He's the *last* person who would be a terrorist!"

Dianne handed them a local newspaper and magazine article about DWF that one of the INS officers read through. He looked up and said reflectively, "Yes. This looks like a false alarm."

Dianne, being a spirited and protective lady, gave the officers quite a hard time. "In the future, just ask the receptionist before rushing in and frightening everyone!"

I have no way for sure of knowing who alerted the INS, but it was too much of a coincidence with the police officer's warning three days earlier. Part of me was disappointed that I wasn't there to meet them. The other part of me was relieved. At that time my perception of any such investigation was that you may not have too many rights until you can clearly prove your innocence. Even though I had evidence and public articles about DWF, it could still have taken some explaining to suspicious INS officers.

The Route

Before finishing work in January 2002, I spent many enjoyable hours working out my route. I studied previous world flight routes (using www.earthrounders.com), researched where aviation gas was available and balanced these with where I really wanted to visit.

The final plan was to pass through 22 countries. The first section crossed the North Atlantic via Canada, Greenland, Iceland and Scotland. The next section passed through France and the Mediterranean via the Islands of Malta, Crete and Cyprus. This was not the most direct route from the U.K. to the Middle East, but I was keen to revisit Malta having been there 17 years earlier, and then explore the other Mediterranean Islands that I'd never been to. The Middle East included Jordan, Bahrain and Oman. Then on to India and the Far East, including Thailand where I stopped for a couple of weeks. Then to Singapore, Indonesia and Australia before hopping across vast expanses of the Pacific Ocean via the islands of New Caledonia, Fiji, Samoa, Christmas Island (in the territory of Kiribati) and Hawaii. This route also passed over the airspace of Italy, Lebanon, Syria, Saudi Arabia and Myanmar (formerly known as Burma). The longest flight was between Hawaii and San Francisco, 2026 nautical miles in total.

I love traveling. There were 11 countries en-route that I had not visited before. I would be armed with *Lonely Planet Guides*, learning and exploring whenever possible. The whole trip was enormously appealing.

At the time of planning, tensions were increasing over Iraq, and I decided to have a contingency plan to avoid the Middle East in case military action broke out. The alternative route was from the U.S. down to Recife on Brazil's east coast, across the South Atlantic to Africa's Ivory Coast, Kenya, across the Indian Ocean to The Seychelles and Sri Lanka before joining the original route in Thailand. This route would have added many miles and I would have missed the U.K., my home country that was extremely important for me to pass through. There were also stories of administrative hassles for light aircraft flying over Africa, such as being refused permission to land. I only wanted to use this contingency route as a last resort.

Concerns

Naturally there are safety issues associated with a light aircraft flight that covers huge tracts of ocean and remote, inaccessible areas. I was concerned specifically about engine reliability over oceans, flying the inhospitable North Atlantic, plus thunderstorms in the tropics. I was also concerned about the Middle East situation. I knew that there would be many unknowns, and ultimately, I wanted to survive this adventure.

I tried to make sure that the plane was in good shape, well maintained and fully serviced. The riskiest scenario would be an engine failure during the first five hours of a flight with full ferry tanks. The aircraft would be up to 20% above its normal maximum weight, and the remaining engine's power would only allow a controlled descent to water or land below.

The recent Twin Comanche belly landing and pilot's death lingered in my mind. I spoke to a few people about that belly landing, and eventually formulated a contingency plan. If we crashed on land, there were few options—your luck has basically run out. However, over water, you have a better chance of surviving. (Recent statistics outlined that 87% of people survive a light aircraft ditching, but that is without those ferry tanks.) Fortunately the vast majority of time when my ferry tanks would be full was over the Pacific Ocean. Just before touching down, the best thing to do would be to try to dip one wing into the water and establish a lateral spin. As the aircraft spun around, the energy in the heavy gas tanks would offset to one side and then to the rear as the aircraft decelerated. It would require some fine judgment, but it was possible. An Australian ferry pilot had recently survived a Beech Bonanza ditching in the Pacific Ocean using this technique. I made sure that any time the aircraft was significantly overweight, the first few hours (while the extra gas was being burned off) would *always* be in daylight. Chances of surviving such a ditching in the dark would be much reduced.

I was also aware that if an engine broke down somewhere remote like Samoa or Kiribati in the middle of the Pacific Ocean, it could trigger a major delay. There would be huge costs incurred in transporting spare parts and a U.S.-qualified engineer to make on-site repairs.

I carried out a full annual inspection before the flight started and changed the engine oil every 50 hours en-route—in the U.K., Thailand, Australia and Hawaii. I also carried out 100-hour engine checks in Thailand and Hawaii. Before starting, I replaced several items that looked (or sounded) like they were worn, such as the auxiliary fuel pumps on both engines, the brake pads and tires. I found a tiny leak in a fuel tank and fixed this. I flew my plane for more than 100 hours around the U.S. before starting, allowing enough time to fix any minor items that went wrong. During this time, an engine oil hose broke loose and sprayed oil inside the engine bay before landing. Had this happened on a long over-water flight, the oil would have drained out, and it would have been necessary to shut down the engine before it seized.

I was lucky. My Baron behaved herself (almost) impeccably while en-route. Only minor items broke down, such as a vacuum pump (for the flight instruments—a second one kicked in as soon as one failed) that was replaced in Thailand. Halfway through the project, the right engine starter-clutch began to make a grinding noise, and it was eventually fixed in Hawaii. In the 200 hours I flew after finishing DWF, a number of things broke down that would have been a nightmare to fix while en-route. I was definitely lucky.

Another concern was flying the inhospitable North Atlantic in autumn. The dangers attached to the North Atlantic (flights from Canada to Europe via Greenland and Iceland) are well known in the flying community. It is a harsh, cold environment. Even in summer, the weather can turn nasty. By autumn the weather is unpredictable and changeable, with sea fog developing suddenly and airframe icing being a real danger. Winter would be bitterly cold. Many light aircraft have been lost to icing and bad weather over the North Atlantic.

If a ditching or crash landing happens, a pilot is faced with surviving in bitterly cold water or on remote and inhospitable land. As a result, Canadian authorities require pilots to wear immersion suits while flying over the North Atlantic region and to carry a sturdy dinghy and a locator beacon that can alert rescue services via satellite. I needed to carry full survival kit, including 10,000 calories of food per person, adequate water supply, cold weather sleeping bags, fishing kit, matches and an axe.

Airframe icing is probably the most dangerous hazard, forming in cloud between freezing level and around $-10°F$. Ice can form on leading edges of the wings, tail plane, windscreen and propellers. It can also form on the propeller blades and engine air intake, reducing power significantly, even choking it off altogether. As ice builds up on the airframe, the aircraft gets heavier and the aerodynamic performance reduces. In plain language, it stops flying. If it is clear ice, which occurs with freezing rain, this can happen terrifyingly fast. An iced-up tail-plane can stall as you reduce speed, particularly dangerous as you slow down before landing. And of course, being heavier you *will* slow down, particularly if the engine output has been reduced and the propellers are generating less thrust. Sadly, over the years icing has led to many fatal crashes.

I therefore looked for an aircraft with de-icing kit. This is comprised of rubber "boots" on the leading edges of the wings and tail-plane with ridges that inflate and, all being well, break off any ice that has accumulated. The aircraft also needed alcohol props and an alcohol windscreen, each having a flow of alcohol that can help prevent or melt icing. (A heated windscreen was too expensive.) Even with boots and alcohol systems, it is illegal to fly into *known* icing conditions. (A heated windscreen is required for legal entry.) These systems are really designed to allow time to exit icing conditions. You can try to do this by descending into warmer (above freezing) temperatures or climbing into cooler temperatures or above the clouds. You can also turn around and fly back out of the icing conditions.

Clearly the best way to reduce the North Atlantic risk was to avoid bad weather and icing conditions. Ideally I wanted to depart by the end of July, so that I could fly during summer months when blocking high pressure weather systems can dominate and make weather conditions stable and good.

I read several articles and watched videos on the subject of icing. I also contacted Ed Carlson who runs an excellent North Atlantic ground school for light aircraft pilots. I couldn't attend his one-day course but bought and read his notes avidly. I spoke with Ed several times over the telephone. He was immensely helpful and pointed out some of the dangers attached, what to look out for and what to avoid. I also got much of the survival kit from Ed.

Looking further ahead to the tropics, I was aware that thunderstorms could be common in the region's moist, warm and unstable air. Thunderstorms have powerful updrafts and downdrafts that can toss a light aircraft around like a leaf in an autumn gale. Light aircraft have been known to break up if caught inside a storm. In Thailand some rainy-season storms would roar through Bangkok, thunder and lightning exploding like battle-field mortar bombs. I had much respect. They were enough to keep you off the streets, let alone fly anywhere near them.

In commercial aircraft, you are usually high enough to avoid bad weather. Some tropical storms can tower up to 60,000 feet, and even commercial airliners have to take avoiding action. In a light aircraft with normally aspirated engines (non-turbocharged), you're lucky to climb to half the height of an average thunderstorm. My Baron was capable of climbing to 18,600 feet, so I would have to go around storms.

To reduce the risk of battling a thunderstorm, I looked for a plane with airborne weather radar that detects rainfall up to 120 miles ahead. This can differentiate rain intensity, detecting heavy falls that can be associated with thunderstorms. I would be able to steer around the heavy *returns* on the screen. This would be particularly useful if flying in cloud with embedded thunderstorms waiting to swallow you up and spit you out.

Flying My Own Plane

I had often dreamed as a young lad of owning my own plane but never thought that I would. Owning and flying a sleek, powerful twin was exciting. In the first two weeks, I flew N30TB over 60 hours and began to get a feel for her. She had a distinctively throaty growl while taxiing, and when airborne, she purred along reassuringly at 175 knots on 65% power at 6,000 feet, burning around 26 gallons of gas per hour.

She was nice to handle; wingovers were a treat. She seemed stable during instrument flying, and she was light and easy to land. Takeoff was positive, accelerating quickly to 80 knots before raising the nose and climbing at 100 knots and around 1,500 feet per minute. I loved having retractable gear again—the last times had been in Australia in 2001, and the RAF almost 14 years earlier.

I installed a second GPS system, a Garmin 430 that had an excellent moving map display and logical data input and management. This proved to be a joy to use, making navigation much easier and worth every extra dollar spent. The GPS was coupled to the autopilot, so once the flight-plan data was punched in, the aircraft would cruise herself to the required destination. Older Barons did not have shoulder harnesses, and I was concerned about this. If ditching in water, sharp deceleration could result in the pilot's head bashing against the instrument panel and control wheel. Trapped in a sinking airplane is not a good time to be slumped unconscious. I was horrified to discover that shoulder harnesses cost $4,000 to install. However, it was worth every extra dollar, for safety and survival's sake.

The downside to owning your own plane is the expense. Strict maintenance requirements must be followed, otherwise the airplane will be non-airworthy—illegal to fly. The pitot-static system (used for the airspeed indicator, altimeter and vertical speed indicator instruments) and transponder need to be checked every two years along with an emergency locator beacon (triggered by deceleration during a crash). Every year an *annual* inspection is necessary. In 2002 a Baron's annual cost around $2,400 assuming nothing was found wrong. The engine oil and filters need to be changed every 50 hours, and 100-hour checks, similar to annual checks, are recommended. The plane needs to be in a hangar and insured. Spare parts and repairs are expensive. Repairs can also take up precious time when you cannot fly your plane. It can be extremely frustrating. Every now and then an *airworthiness directive* (AD) circulates from the FAA, and owners are required to comply. It can cost several thousand dollars to fix or replace a defective part. The risk of this is the owner's. The original manufacturer is not normally responsible for the cost of complying with an AD.

The upside of having your own plane is that you have sole access to it. It's your pride and joy. You can get attached to your plane. I've had the pleasure of flying N30TB around the world. She's my "metallic girlfriend."

Flying Incidents

With over 300 hours of flying training and preparations, I was not surprised to experience an incident or two before starting DWF. Indeed, I experienced two, both of which occurred during a long flight of 1,200 nautical miles from Omaha to San Francisco in September—nine hours flying time.

The San Francisco flight was split into two sections, one from Omaha to Rock Springs, Wyoming, where I refueled, and the other from Rock Springs to Hayward Executive Airport in San Francisco, originally planned via Salt Lake City. The flight to Rock Springs was uneventful, although clouds were beginning to build over the Rockies by the time I landed. On the ground, the FBO attendant filled the gas tanks while I got an updated weather briefing inside for the onward flight. I discovered that icing conditions were forecast in cloud around the Salt Lake Valley. I therefore planned a detour well to the south to avoid this area.

At 14,000 feet in cloud over the Utah Mountains, autopilot engaged, I was *head down* checking engine instruments and watching the GPS navigation profile. Suddenly I heard a distinct *swish* followed by a gradual slowing from 145 knots indicated airspeed to 120 knots. I looked out and saw thick ice on the leading edges of the wings and elevators, and on the windshield. It had increased the weight of the plane and slowed her down. The HF aerial (a plastic-covered wire running from the top of the fuselage to the left wing tip) was also encrusted in ice, and flapping wildly in the airflow.

Jet Provost TMk5 trainer in close formation, U.K., 1986

Advanced Flying Training Course-mates by Hawk jet, Wales, 1987 (from left: Jon May, Wayne H, Steve W-S, Al B, Gary Waterfall, Douglas, Keith Collister, Dave B)

"Wings" graduation day with my parents, RAF Valley, Wales, 1987

A few years later, 63 Basic Flying Training Course reunion, U.K., 2001 (back row from left; Al B, Douglas, Jon May, Gordo H, Simon P, front row from left; Colin B, Rich Watson, Steve W-S, Steve H)

Microlight flying - friend Philip at the controls, Thailand, 2000

Setting off on Australia tour, Melbourne, Australia, 2001 with (left to right) Gillem, Noirin, Liz and Hugh

Flying N30TB over cornfields of Iowa, U.S., August 2002

Diabetes World Flight departure day, Omaha, U.S., 24 September 2002

With safety pilot James, near Boston, U.S.

Fiord with icebergs below, near Narsarsuaq, Greenland

Narsarsuaq final approach with glacier in distance, Greenland

Fiords and glaciers, eastern Greenland

Fort William (my home town) basking in the rain! Scotland

Cockpit at 11,000 feet en-route Crete, Greece

Island of Crete coastline and mountains, Greece

With Ty, floating high in the Dead Sea, Jordan

Medicinal Mud, Dead Sea, Jordan

Petra's ancient "Treasury Building,"
hewn out of rock, Jordan

Filling ferry tanks before 6 hour flight over the Middle East

Mahalaxmi Dhobi Ghat, Mumbai's municipal laundry, India

Mid-flight over Myanmar (Burma) (wearing pilot uniforms made airport arrival & departure formalities easier in the Middle East and Asia)

Low approach runway 23, Bangphra, Thailand

Final approach into Phuket, Thailand (where tsunamis struck in December 2004)

Uluru (Ayres Rock) – sacred ground to the Aboriginal people – in the distance, Northern Territory, Australia

Glasshouse Mountain, Queensland, Australia

With Angus and Gem Hutton, and dog "Sir Joh," (with type 1 diabetes), Gympie Airport, Queensland, Australia

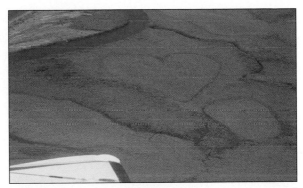

"La Coeur du Voh" heart outline in 100% natural vegetation, New Caledonia

With Dr. Satu Viali (right) and Asomahiu Tupuala at Samoa's only diabetes clinic

Christmas Island's Air Traffic Controller helping out after our "early arrival"

Ty and Maria's wedding, Hawaii

North coast of Kauai, Hawaii

Humpback whales off south coast of Molokai, Hawaii

Kilauea volcano on "The Big Island," Hawaii

The ferry tanks (on right) after being dismantled, Hayward Airport, San Francisco, U.S.

Finished! Day 159, Council Bluffs Airport near Omaha, 19 February, 2003

Uh Oh! This icing had happened incredibly quickly, most likely in a shower of freezing rain. I immediately cycled the de-ice boots, watching the rubber seals inflate and gradually deflate to their smooth profile 30 seconds later. Only a portion of ice broke off. I switched on the de-ice alcohol for the propellers and windscreen. As the alcohol streamed over the lower portion of the windscreen, a small hole cleared. I could just see out of this peephole, but only into dull gray cloud. At this time the HF aerial was flapping so wildly I was worried that it might break its wing-tip anchor. If this happened, it could possibly wrap around the rudder, impeding rudder (yaw) and even elevator (pitch) control. Not good.

Flying in icing conditions, in cloud and above high mountains is a bad place to be. I considered the options. Turning around and back into *known* icing, would be a bad idea, and illegal. No further ice was accumulating, and clear weather was forecast ahead. The only option was to press on ahead. However, two minutes later, I heard a second *swish* and in an instant, another thick crusting of ice appeared. I recycled the de-ice boots again, but only patches on the wing's leading edge cleared.

I sat there thinking about the situation. In some conditions, icing can build up so quickly that it can bring a light plane down within minutes, even seconds. In this case, the build-up had been incredibly fast, with two bursts of a few seconds. If I encountered much more, I would be in big trouble, slowly descending over the cloud-covered Utah Mountains.

Imagine my great relief when the cloud gradually brightened, and within 20 minutes, the clouds had cleared. My respect for icing was confirmed. This experience emphasized the importance of an escape plan when flying the North Atlantic—ideally having warm (above-freezing) temperatures to descend safely into, should we encounter icing.

I was interested to see what my blood sugar level was. It was definitely a stressful few moments, and the adrenaline could easily push blood sugars higher. However, they were not abnormally high over the remaining hour of flight to San Francisco.

While cruising at 14,000 feet for almost three hours, I had been using a portable oxygen tank with cannula tubing in my nostrils. Oxygen is required by regulations if you are flying above 12,500 feet for more than half an hour. Shortly before descending into Hayward, and a good hour after the icing incident, I felt mildly nauseated. I reasoned that this could be hypoxia, so I checked the oxygen tubing, connections and oxygen flow meter. Everything appeared to be normal. I had just tested my blood sugar a short time before. However, I tested again. Nausea can also be a symptom of hypoglycemia. My blood sugar test was well above 100 mg. All fine here, too.

A couple of minutes into the descent toward Hayward, I began to feel fine again and didn't think any more of it. When stowing the oxygen equipment at Hayward, I noticed a plastic join halfway along the 2 meters of tubing that was disconnected. I had missed this connection point when checking earlier. The penny dropped. I had probably been suffering mild hypoxia when I felt slightly nauseated. In future I would check more carefully—right along the whole length of tubing when using it. And even if nothing appeared wrong, check it again.

Chapter:

8 Around the World in 159 Days

*...let us hope that the advent of a successful flying machine,
now only dimly foreseen and nevertheless thought to be possible,
will bring nothing but good into the world; that it shall
abridge distance, make all parts of the globe accessible, bring
men into closer relation with each other, advance civilization,
and hasten the promised era in which there shall be nothing
but peace and good will among men.*

—Octave Chanute, 1894

The Adventure Begins

On September 24, 2002, everything was in place: the ferry tanks, HF radio
and a new GPS navigation system. N30TB was fresh from her annual inspection. Even though I had replaced several mechanical components, I had a
spare vacuum pump (for instrumentation) and alternator on board, kindly
donated by Harold Cheeseman of Omaha Airplane Supply. I had all the
charts and maps required for flights to the East Coast, plus Jeppessen Trip Kit
charts for the North Atlantic crossing as far as Iceland. My two GPS systems
had updated chips for the U.S. and Europe. The plane had all its required
registration and radio license documents for international flights, and my
own licenses (including a radio license) were all in order for a solo flight
around the world.

Two months earlier I'd gained my instrument rating *add on* for twin engine aircraft and had since flown over 50 hours with Brian to become familiar with the U.S. IFR (instrument) flying system. (When you gain your IFR rating it's really just the beginning—you keep on learning and gaining valuable experience the more you fly.) Since the start of the year, I'd logged 309 hours, including two flights in the Baron from Omaha to San Francisco, and one to Cape Cod on the East Coast and back. I felt comfortable with long distance flights. I was happy with my blood sugar control. I'd flown almost 500 hours using the U.S. system for pilots with diabetes in the previous three years and found it safe and practical to use.

A few days earlier, I had been touched when Eileen Smith at Council Bluffs Airport gave me a St. Joseph's Prayer card. She told me that I would not suffer a "violent death" or "burn to death" if I carried this prayer card. Even though I am not Catholic, I was happy to have St. Joseph along with me on this adventure.

The last few days of preparations were hectic. Edleman sent out media alerts and press releases, and three television stations and two newspapers came out to interview me at Council Bluffs Airport. Roche Diagnostics had donated three Accu-Chek Compact meters with test drums. I resolved to keep at least two meters and plenty of test strips available in the cockpit at all times. I would also keep plenty of carbohydrates available.

It was a hot, sunny day with unrestricted visibility (clear skies), a perfect day for departure. The media teams gave quick interviews and televised my first pre-flight blood sugar test. It was 169, well within the 100–300 mg/dl required for flying, and within my personal flying target of 100–170.

At 3:30 p.m. I climbed aboard N30TB. It was an emotional moment, the culmination of five intense months of preparations. It was finally happening. I had no idea how it would all work out. Would the aircraft be reliable? Would I run into bad weather? Would I cross the North Atlantic safely? Indeed, would I survive this trip should an engine quit when we were overweight with extra gas over the Pacific Ocean? It was a great step into the unknown. I felt I could have done with another month to polish off preparations, but enough had been done. It was time to go!

Even though my pre-flight test was 169, I thought my blood sugar could be lowering. I popped a solid peppermint candy into my mouth and started to chew as I was taxiing to runway 13. A few seconds later I felt a loud crunch! *Damn!* In the excitement, I had been chewing hard and broken a filling. Was this an omen? It would certainly require a visit to the dentist the next day. I decided to forget about it and enjoy the departure.

I took off at precisely 3:40 p.m., climbed to 800 feet above ground and turned downwind for a low pass over runway 13. Flying 30 feet above the runway at 180 knots (207 mph) was definitely the best way to start DWF! I pulled up and banked eastward, and while climbing to 2,000 feet, I pushed the transmit button and broadcast on ground frequency, "See you in five months."

A couple of minutes later to the east, Mark Borman was flying his dad's Baron B58 with Brian, my instructor for the summer, plus two friends, Dave (an air traffic controller at Omaha Approach) and Lori, on board. I joined up beside him and for 15 minutes we reveled in close formation flying, wheeling around while Dave took photos. I could have carried on doing this for ages, but a four-hour flight to Cleveland lay ahead. We bid each other farewell, and I turned N30TB to the east for the first leg of this 26,000-mile journey. Climbing to 7,000 feet, I activated the instrument flight plan with Omaha Approach on frequency 124.5. Dave had been working that morning at Omaha Approach, and saw my flight plan details printing out from the computer. He had added a note in the *Remarks* section of the flight plan: *First leg of round the world flight.* While I was flying toward Cleveland, two air traffic controllers saw the note and asked what the world flight was all about. It was a nice touch.

The four-hour flight to Cuyahoga County Airport, Cleveland, was spent in crystal-clear conditions. I took six blood sugar tests during the flight. The lowest was 103 mg/dl and the highest 176. I was extremely happy flying along at 175 knots in my twin-engine machine. (I was getting to know my metallic girlfriend well—and liked her a lot.) As I continued eastward, Chicago's skyline was silhouetted against a crimson sunset, a stunning sight. As darkness fell, the lights of towns twinkled ahead in the distance. Cleveland soon lit up the sky ahead, and I made a speedy descent over Lake Huron into Cuyahoga Airport.

An hour after landing, I checked into a nearby Holiday Inn Express and enjoyed a quiet beer and snack at the bar. I talked with two cheerful guys who ended up donating $20 to diabetes research. Later, I reflected on the day's activities. This day had been a tremendous start to my dream to fly around the world. However, I needed to visit a dentist the next morning.

North Atlantic

While I wanted to meet with diabetes associations and people with diabetes in as many countries as possible, initially I just wanted to focus on crossing the North Atlantic safely. I resolved to be disciplined about weather conditions and not to take any unnecessary risks.

Hurricane Isidore had just ravaged Cuba and some U.S. Gulf states. It was now an intense depression passing northward along the East Coast. I had to be careful about Isidore. In Mansfield near Boston, its appalling weather resulted in 200-foot cloud bases, heavy rain and poor visibility and delayed me by one day.

James Aiden, the British safety pilot, joined me in Mansfield. I was extremely busy in the local Holiday Inn, planning each flight ahead as far as Iceland, writing the website journal, arranging permission to fly into Iceland with ferry tanks, catching up on my DWF accounts, and contacting diabetes associations in the countries ahead.

During the bad weather day, I was quite stressed with all the organizing and ate too much carbohydrate at lunchtime. By mid-afternoon my blood sugar had risen to 300. I was horrified and really angry with myself for the lack of discipline. This was one of the highest sugars I'd had since being diagnosed. Immediately I topped up with an injection of short-acting insulin, and 30 minutes later (after the insulin began to take effect) went for an energetic swim in the indoor pool. I swam for ages, and a couple of hours later, was much happier to see sugar levels back down to normal.

There were four flights over the North Atlantic route: Bangor to Goose Bay, on to Narsarsuaq in Greenland, then to Reykjavik in Iceland and, finally, on to Inverness in Scotland, just 50 miles from where my parents live. First, James and I had to fly to Bangor from Boston.

On September 28, the weather had cleared for the short flight to Bangor, Maine at 9,000 feet. My pre-flight sugar test was 113, and during the flight, two tests were 200 and 207, a bit higher than I normally wanted for flying, but bang in the middle of the required range of 100–300 for flying. James was fun to fly with. He offered to change radio frequencies for me, but I declined. This would be in keeping with the solo nature of the world flight.

The following day we flew from Bangor to Goose Bay, my first international flight. Goose Bay sat 607 nautical miles to the north and took exactly four hours to reach. We caught glimpses of barren and uninhabited Canadian

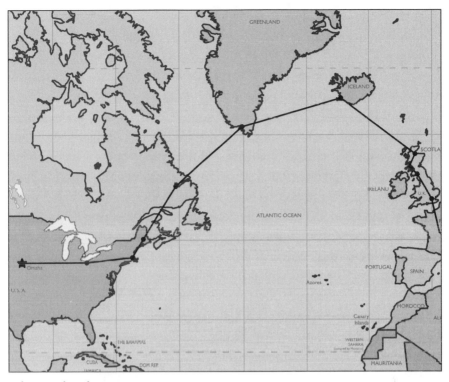

The North Atlantic

countryside between individual cumulus clouds below. It looked remote down there. In the last hour, the cloud thickened to 8/8 cover with tops gradually rising to meet us. When cleared to descend, almost immediately we entered turbulent cloud where sleet and snow produced thick ice on the wings and tail. The HF aerial flapped like a sheet in a force 9 gale. I cycled the de-ice boots and switched on the windscreen and propellers alcohol system.

Cycling the boots only broke off part of the ice. The good thing was that we could descend below freezing level at around 2,000 feet. First we had to clear the northern edge of the Mealy Mountains. The HF aerial was flapping so wildly, I decided to test a theory. If someone touches the HF aerial during transmission, they will receive a burn. I wondered whether the aerial would heat up during transmitting and melt the ice, so I dialed in a random frequency and transmitted. The theory didn't work. The aerial remained coated with thick ice. This multi-tasking took my full attention off the instruments, and my rate of descent in cloud had slowed up. *Fly the plane, stupid!* We needed to keep going down into warmer air.

Soon we broke through the cloud, and the ice gradually melted. *Good.* Goose Bay lay ahead in dull, gray conditions. It was cold and damp on the ground, and N30TB was stored in the hangar in case of snowfall that night. It was quite strange to be here. When I was in the RAF, colleagues used to come here on fast-jet training detachments. Had I not been diagnosed with diabetes, I could well have been here before.

The next day was spent on the ground while former Tropical Storm Isidore sat to the west of southern Greenland as a deep low-pressure system. This is exactly what Ed Carlson's ground school had warned against. When low pressure systems lie to the west, low clouds and fog can form quickly and drift up the fiord on the west coast, making landing potentially dangerous, if not impossible at Narsarsuaq. Other airports on the west coast of Greenland would likely be in the same condition. I heeded the advice "Don't go until the depression moves to the east of Greenland" when weather should be more stable.

By the 1st of October the low pressure system had moved eastward and opened up a *weather window.* At 8 a.m. sharp, James and I arrived at Goose Bay Airport. However, the FBO had not brought N30TB out of the hanger as requested. This was frustrating. After 3:30 p.m. at Narsarsuaq the landing fee shot up from $200 to $600. I literally couldn't afford a major delay. While N30TB was being towed out of the hanger, a charter plane taxied in and the FBO surprisingly decided to refuel this plane ahead of ours. James was so frustrated, he forced himself to sit in a quiet room to one side. The charter plane took 30 minutes to refuel, after which it took a further 30 minutes to fill N30TB's main tanks and put 60 gallons into the ferry tanks. I was distinctly unimpressed with this FBO. However, when we eventually finished, we had enough gas for 8 hours flying time and just enough time to avoid the expensive landing fee.

At least the delay gave me more time to study the weather forecast. Weather en-route was mixed, with broken cloud at 5,000 feet for 200 miles, a weak warm front for another 250 miles with broken cloud at 2,000 all the way up to 12,000 feet and then 15,000 feet. Moderate icing was forecast in cloud in temperatures below freezing. The final 150 miles the forecast was for broken cloud at 2,000 feet while Narsarsuaq had broken cloud at 3,500 feet and scattered clouds at 8,000. Freezing level was 2,000 feet. This looked promising. I planned to start out at 7,000 feet and climb above cloud near the warm front. If we couldn't climb high and encountered icing, we had an escape route—descend into warm and clear air below 2,000 feet. I planned to descend below cloud about 50 miles off the coast of Greenland where we would fly a visual approach up a 40-mile fiord into Narsarsuaq. I filed the flight plan, did a pre-flight walk-around check of the plane, and then we donned our immersion suits for the first time.

The immersion suits were uncomfortable. They were bulky and impeded movement in the cockpit. I couldn't wear shoes, which felt odd in an aircraft. We pulled the suits up to our waists and left the upper section unzipped between our backs and the seat, the suit arms squashed up against the side of the cockpit. If we were unfortunate enough to lose an engine and ditch, we would have to pull our suit arms on and zip up during descent (a difficult task). I was concerned that the immersion suit would restrict my left hand and arm movement for operating the control yoke, but when push came to shove, I didn't even notice.

My pre-flight blood sugar test was 263, horribly high for me, but okay for flying. The stress of the delay and some apprehension about this long flight over chilly waters was probably responsible. I quickly topped up with some short-acting insulin.

After takeoff, it was beautifully clear as we flew along a fiord toward the Labrador Sea. Soon clouds began to build, though, triggering a climb to 10,000 feet. However, more cloud rose sharply before us, and light icing began to build up before we could climb above. At 12,500 it was clear. *Good.* As we were coasting offshore, we could hear air traffic control (ATC) giving HF frequencies to call Gander Radio. We could hear plenty of transmissions but none of our transmissions seemed to get through. The radio frequencies were incredibly busy with cross-Atlantic airliner traffic. Every now and then satellite telephone frequencies would come through, distinct two-tones ringing in our ears. You had to be quick to squeeze any radio calls in. Gander eventually responded with "November Three Zero Tango Bravo, you are barely readable."

Each hour you are required to give your call sign, position, time (in Hours Zulu), flight level or height, next position, estimated time of next position, and finally the subsequent position. If we couldn't do this directly with Gander radio, we could try relaying our position on emergency guard frequency of 121.5 to airliners passing overhead.

We tried a number of alternative HF frequencies before making calls on 121.5. However, nobody passed by close enough to pick up our VHF broadcast. I was aware that after one hour of no contact as expected from us, search and rescue would be alerted. Eventually we relayed a position report with Delta 49 passing 20,000 feet above us.

Just over 120 miles from Greenland's coastline, I contacted Narsarsuaq Information frequency for updated weather and altimeter setting. Narsarsuaq's weather was good—broken cloud at 2,500 feet and a ceiling of 4,500 feet. However, thick cloud continued ahead of us at 12,000 feet. At 50 miles offshore, as planned, I descended to look for clear air below 2,000 feet. As per the forecast, on reaching 2,000 feet the cloud was thinning, and we could see water below. However, the cloud base continued to lower. I descended further, but even at 500 feet above sea level, cloud was lowering and visibility deteriorating. The weather was distinctly worse than forecast. *Damn!* I was really hoping to enjoy a visual approach along picturesque fiords of Greenland. If this low cloud unexpectedly continued all along the fiord to Narsarsuaq, we would have to make the instrument approach. And the start height would most likely be in icing layers. *Not good.*

We descended lower, and I checked with James that he was comfortable with our height and marginal visibility. He said he was. However, visibility decreased further and below us sat banks of sea fog. It wasn't long before I felt pretty uncomfortable myself, and as I initiated a climb away from the water, James said pensively, "Hmm. There's an iceberg below us!"

I dug out the Narsarsuaq instrument plate (chart) and started to study it in preparation for an approach. Suddenly, we burst out of cloud into beautiful clear air. *Eureka!* Breathtaking views of Greenland's coastline and fiords lay before us. It was terrific. We could carry out a visual approach after all. It was time to relax and really enjoy the last 20 minutes of this flight.

At 1,000 feet, we flew along a fiord (sea loch) between steep-sided mountains. Below us chunks of ice and icebergs bobbed gently in the water. I was struck by how similar this landscape is to the Scottish Highlands, but with one huge difference—there are no icebergs floating in Scottish sea lochs! After a brief moment of confusion over which fiord to turn down, we cruised by a fishing settlement at the water's edge. Multi-colored wooden houses dotted this remote township whose only access was by sea.

We continued to fly along the steep-sided fiord, following as it gradually curved to the left. As the fiord straightened, I saw the beginning of a runway angled off to the right—Narsarsuaq Airfield. Broken clouds clung to the hillsides at 2,000 feet, while a large towering cumulus rose directly above the airfield. Turning right between the mountains we lined up on runway 7. A glacier glinted in the distance, snaking its way down the valley toward us. Behind it were high mountains backing onto what looked like a wall of ice. It was a beautiful backdrop. With a light tailwind, our ground speed was high on touchdown. However, runway 7 sloped steeply uphill, and we decelerated quickly.

It felt good to arrive in one piece. I had been concerned about this leg, with its potential icing, unpredictable weather and cold, remote geography. I took four blood sugar tests on the flight from Goose Bay to Narsarsuaq. After the high start of 263, it reduced to 187 and 126 before increasing to 247 before landing. I wondered if the excitement (stress) of the last hour was enough to push sugar this high in such a short period of time. It was quite possible, especially combined with a sweet crispy bar I ate just before descent.

Narsarsuaq base is an old World War II staging post used for ferrying aircraft from the U.S. to the U.K. It is now comprised of the runway, airport buildings, a hotel, some workers' accommodation blocks, equipment shelters and an old U.S. army hospital further up the valley. The Narsarsuaq people seemed relaxed and friendly, making for an enjoyable stopover.

The following morning, low clouds and mist brushed through the valley for most of the morning, delaying our departure. Perhaps this was the sea fog we encountered the day before, now pushing its way east. Any potential frustration was soon defused by chatting with Jens, an animated and entertaining Greenland Air Dash 7 Captain. We had watched him descending steeply into Narsarsuaq in very marginal weather conditions. When he climbed down from the cockpit, he was singing Freddie Mercury's *We are the Champions!* at the top of his voice. Here was a guy clearly satisfied with his instrument flying skills!

We chatted with Jens for an hour by which time conditions were improving. My blood sugar was 111—perfect. We pulled on our immersion suits and got ready for departure. Immediately after takeoff from down-sloping runway 25, we had to take a sharp right turn followed by a left turn to intercept an outgoing bearing from a navigation beacon. I had studied this procedure and the visual charts the previous night. I wanted to know where the mountains were. We soon climbed into cloud, and for a few moments, I drifted off course—not a good idea on this departure. We burst above clouds at 5,000 feet into clear sunshine and stunning views of fiords off to the distant west

On turning right to the east, we were amazed by the sight of Greenland's ice-cap as it rose to 9,000 feet before us. We tracked over this enormous ice monolith stretching to the horizon, punctuated occasionally by *nunataks*—mountain peaks piercing though the ice. I had studied glacial morphology at Edinburgh University, and this was an awe-inspiring example.

As we approached the east coast of Greenland, we drank in views of ice-filled fiords and huge icebergs floating in cold coastal waters. An hour later we could still see mountains 200 miles to the north. The air was incredibly clear.

Conditions for the rest of this 667-mile journey remained clear except for one small detour around some towering cumulus clouds. These can be extremely turbulent inside, so it is best to avoid them. My first in-flight blood sugar test was 223, very high for me but fine for flying. Most likely a sweet rice-crisp snack before takeoff was responsible, possibly combined with a little stress during the instrument departure. I topped up with fast-acting insulin. The next tests were 225 and 201. Although this was fine for flying, it was still high for me, so I topped up again.

It had been raining in Reykjavik, but only a thin layer of stratocumulus cloud interrupted our VOR instrument approach. In perfectly calm conditions and with a thin film of water on the runway, we hardly even noticed the touchdown. It was a rare silky-smooth landing. James mockingly exclaimed, "You're just taking the piss!" (My good buddy Gillem would have lambasted this smoother-than-my-average landing as "level 9 on the Richter Scale" but as pilots may say, "Any landing you walk away from is a good one.")

In many respects, the landing at Reykjavik completed the first stage of DWF. We had passed the bulk of the cold, inhospitable North Atlantic safely. It had been an exciting few days. I had been stressed at times with planning and avoiding weather risks. While I'd had some high blood sugars for me, they were all comfortably within the required range for FAA blood sugar testing. I was pleased with progress so far.

Iceland—First Diabetes Association Meeting

One thing I learned was that Iceland's autumn weather is as wet and windy as the weather in northwest Scotland! Conditions were disgusting for three days, and at one point, I was genuinely worried about the plane sitting in the open at the airport in winds of more than 40 knots.

I met with Kim Mortensen, one of the trustees of the Iceland Diabetes Association. Kim took James and me on a marathon 300-km tour of Iceland's stunning volcanic scenery, geothermal power station, geysers, waterfalls and historic sites. It was a terrific day out, polished off with Icelandic hospitality, a meal of Icelandic lamb cooked by Kim's wife, Sesseljia.

The picture of diabetes in Iceland displays stark differences from the U.S. and Europe. Out of a population of 285,000, there are only 5,000 people with diabetes. This 2% incidence compares to estimates of 5.7% in the U.S. and 3.8% in the UK. Why would this be? Iceland should share much the same gene pool as their neighbors to the east and west, so what makes the difference? Possibly Iceland's relatively high-fish diet. However, junk food is gaining in popularity, and as a result obesity is becoming more common. Type 2 diabetes usually occurs in middle age, often coinciding with middle-age spread. In turn, the incidence of type 2 diabetes in Iceland is increasing.

The incidence of type 1 diabetes is particularly low, and The University of Iceland is carrying out research on whether milk produced by Iceland's dairy herd might have some preventive quality. This herd has existed in isolation for hundreds of years and according to Darwin's theory of evolution, it's possible that changes (mutations) have occurred that now help prevent type 1 diabetes.

The diabetes association is run by a small group of enthusiastic individuals, nearly all with kids or other family members with diabetes. I joined the association's weekly walk on Sunday and *enjoyed* a brisk jaunt in blustery winds and torrential rain. It was a great way to promote exercise as part of managing diabetes. Icelanders are a hardy lot.

North Atlantic—Final Leg

By Monday, October 7, scudding clouds and torrential rain had given way to calm and dry conditions in Reykjavik. It was a welcome change for the flight to Inverness, Scotland, a 650-nautical mile journey over chilly North Atlantic waters. I had my first taste of foreign media interviews, meeting Omar, a reporter from the government television station. Omar was a well-known character in Iceland who was himself interested in aviation. He had once found himself in trouble for landing a microlight on a nearby mountain peak.

It was a stressful morning, as the Jeppessen Trip Kit for Europe had not been delivered as promised. This had all the charts and instrument approach plates required for our flight that day, and the courier delivery never came. Fortunately my existing North Atlantic chart covered the route, and thankfully the FBO had copies of instrument approach plates for Inverness and two alternative airfields, Wick and Stornoway. We were still in business but somewhat delayed.

My pre-flight blood sugar was 124—great. However, my sugar had gone a little low during the morning, and I had stuffed some rice-crisp bar into my mouth before the interviews. My first in-flight test result was 267, my highest airborne result ever. My body had probably been pumping adrenaline while low and with the stress of the delayed start. I was frustrated with such a high reading. In the cockpit's confined space, I struggled to pull the immersion suit down below waist level, pulled up my under-vests and shirts and exposed some stomach area. The needle went in, and my short-acting insulin top-up was complete. (At that moment in time, an insulin pump would have been handy, with its already attached catheter and tubing allowing a punch of a button and easy delivery of rapid-acting insulin.) I was pleased to see subsequent hourly test results reduce to 225, 170 and 140.

Soon after takeoff, I turned east and climbed to Flight Level 090 (9,000 feet). It was a cloudy, damp day further along the south coast of Iceland, but through some cloud layers, we gained an occasional glimpse of an icecap and mountains to the north. It would have been a beautiful island to fly around in good weather. After an hour we passed through a frontal band of rain, at which point a light layering of ice began to build up on the wings. The temperature had changed at our cruising level. We were soon cleared to descend to 7,000 feet where the air was warmer, and the ice melted off. I was almost getting used to dealing with icing, but my immense respect for its dangers remained.

Strong headwinds slowed our ground speed significantly, and it took five hours to reach Inverness. After two hours, I switched to the ferry tanks. I was now used to rolling the seat back and stretching back into the floor-well behind James to switch levers. The procedure was firmly imprinted on my mind, *Left fuel pump on, left ferry tank lever on, feed lever to the left engine on, wait a few seconds, turn main left tank off, wait 10 seconds and then turn left fuel pump off. If no spluttering from the left engine, fuel flow fine. Now repeat for the right hand side....* If this procedure was not rigidly followed, the engine would be starved of fuel and start coughing and spluttering. I did this once during DWF, resulting in sputtering expletives as my heart leapt to my mouth. The guilty lever was quickly turned back to its proper position, and shortly after, the engine resumed its throaty six-cylinder growl.

Dusk was falling as we approached the north Scottish Highlands. Coming from the north, it was odd to see the GPS map display Scotland upside down. A quick pre-landing test showed 148 mg/dl—*good*—after which I flew an arcing VOR instrument approach into Inverness Airport. I have fond memories of Inverness Airport as the site of my first flying lesson at the age of 18. As soon as we parked and disembarked, a car drove up. My parents were on board, and it was tremendous to see them. I was looking forward to four days of the comforts of home.

I peeled off my immersion suit for the last time and stowed it in the back of the plane. It felt good to complete the North Atlantic crossing, arguably the most dangerous passage of DWF. This was also James' last flight as safety pilot. He had been particularly good company, very relaxed and fun to be with, and I was extremely grateful for his safety pilot duties. It was not the last I'd see of James, however, as he became a valued adviser for the onward U.K. visual (VFR) flights (not using formal instrument flight plans), and he also hosted me at White Waltham Airfield near London.

Scotland—My Home Country

Four days later, I was looking forward to flying over home territory. On October 12, however, the weather forecast was not brilliant, with overcast weather and a small frontal band of rain with low cloud to the southwest of Inverness. The rain was forecast to clear toward Glasgow and Carlisle, today's two destinations.

This was my first flight with Ty, the second safety pilot, who had arrived from Miami the previous day. Ty had never flown outside the U.S., and it had been a long time since I had flown the U.K. system. James Aiden, the first safety pilot, had sent us his visual flying maps, and we spoke at length with him to ensure we wouldn't be making any procedural mistakes or busting airspace unwittingly. The main thing today was having an escape route should the weather clamp down too much. I would pull up into cloud and climb above minimum safety altitude to be clear of mountaintops. I would then call up *Scottish* for a radar service and fly to Prestwick near Glasgow. Ty was amazed that it was legal to do this. In the U.S., it is illegal to fly in cloud unless you are on an instrument flight plan and talking with ATC already.

I loved every single minute of this flight. It was home territory, and after leaving the airport zone, I didn't need to look at a map for another 100 miles. Lifting off Inverness' northerly runway, I turned 180 degrees and departed downwind, straight over Inverness and on to Loch Ness. Not far ahead was a Cessna 152. The Baron was growling along happily at 155 knots, closing in on the Cessna puttering along at 80 knots (at best). I caught him up near Invermoriston where we passed underneath and to the right side. We got fairly close to the hillside doing this—it was the only safe way to pass with the cloud base continually lowering. From a distance the Cessna looked like it was hanging motionless in mid-air. Closer up, our relative speeds were clear to see. We left him in the dust!

There wasn't much dust ahead though, just low cloud and rain. Nearing Fort Augustus, Ty was studying the visual map rather intently. He looked up and observed our increasingly marginal flying conditions and exclaimed, "Flying doesn't come any better than this!" He seemed to love the low flying and the challenge of deteriorating weather conditions in the Highlands of Scotland. I liked his attitude.

For me this was bliss. I was low flying my own plane through the steep-sided glens where I grew up. I had dreamed of doing this as a young lad. If I could have seen myself all those years ahead flying my own Baron down the Great Glen I would have been pretty excited. Had I known *why* I was doing this (diabetes), undoubtedly I would have been upset. But right then, I was happy.

Rather amusingly, the rain was heaviest right over my parents' house on the shores of Loch Lochy. There was some space above so I pulled up and then banked steeply to the left, a classic wing-over, to enjoy the view of my home while reversing direction. This is a pleasant maneuver, with near zero G at the apex of the turn. Ty sensed the change and looked up sharply from his map. He then glanced over to the airspeed indicator on my side of the cockpit, most likely wondering how close we were to stalling speed. As far as I knew, Ty had never carried out such a maneuver in a twin, and I was quietly amused at his reaction. He would have to *endure* a few more of these over the next few months.

I had said goodbye to my parents at Inverness Airport, so they weren't at home to wave oilskins as they'd done 16 years ago at my Jet Provost. A few miles further on at Gairlochy, I banked over my old school buddy's house. However, patches of cloud were appearing *below* us to the east and visibility was markedly reducing, a couple of miles at the most. I wondered whether I would have to exercise the escape plan. However, another 10 miles southwest along the Great Glen, the rain slackened, and I was able to catch a glimpse of Ben Nevis' steep and rocky slopes above us. Visibility then cleared dramatically, shafts of sunlight illuminating Loch Linnhe directly ahead.

As we passed by the picturesque fishing towns of Oban, Crinan and Lochgilphead, we flew over beautifully calm waters and played underneath wispy low clouds. I marveled at the mystical qualities in this view of the Scottish Western Isles. Far into the distance, I could see the Isle of Colonsay basking in cloud-diffused sunlight and mirror-like waters, quite a surreal view.

Just before leaving Loch Linnhe to go on to Glasgow, I tested my blood sugar—126, ideal. I was then into less familiar territory, so I looked at the maps and cross-referred various landmarks with the GPS moving map display. I couldn't help reflecting on how much easier life was with sophisticated GPS systems. Low-level flying in the RAF required a hand-held map and a trusty stopwatch. However, the easier it is, the better and the safer. I appreciated the GPS enormously.

A Trip Down Memory Lane

There is nothing like returning to a place that remains unchanged to find the ways in which you yourself have altered.
—Nelson Mandela

In the U.K., one of my old course mates, Squadron Leader Gary Waterfall, arranged a visit to my first training base, Royal Air Force College Cranwell. This is where we had learned to fly Jet Provosts in 1986 and 1987, and I was to meet with Group Captain Mike Cross OBE RAFC, my old Chief Flying Instructor.

Departing for Cranwell from White Waltham's grass strip, at 40 knots the Baron launched herself off a hidden ridge, and we found ourselves prematurely airborne. I held the yoke back to keep the nose-wheel off the ground and prevent it from digging in as we thumped back down. (I also held my breath.) Once we were properly airborne, it was a beautiful day, with fluffy white cumulus clouds punctuating blue skies. It was exhilarating to fly my own plane over the U.K. The route took us north to the Midlands, squeezing between controlled (and congested) airspace. Fifteen miles out I called up Cranwell ATC and flew over the town of Sleaford before lining up on familiar old runway 27. A tiny single-engine plane descended and flew alongside us, filming for BBC Lincolnshire.

As we taxied in, there was a large group waiting with television cameras and radio recorders. Great stuff! This would be really good for raising awareness of diabetes. I parked N30TB and shut the engines down. Just before opening the door, I jokingly mentioned to Ty that this would be a "great moment" to keel over with a severe hypoglycemic reaction. Ty turned around, and to his credit, looked me straight in the eye and asked, "Are you okay?" He wasn't familiar with my self-deprecating sense of humor. (More to the point, at times the British sense of humor can be quite understated or ironic, something that people from other nations don't always understand.)

"No, it's okay. I'm only joking," was my quick reply.

It was a real pleasure to meet and chat with Mike Cross, the Chief Flying Instructor I'd flown my navigation contest with in 1987. He had been my ultimate boss 15 years earlier, and initially, it felt quite strange to be calling him "Mike" instead of "Sir."

We spent half an hour interviewing with television, radio and newspaper crews. It was cold and when we retired indoors for coffee, Mike quietly told me his amazing story. He had been flying in the RAF with type 1 diabetes, without telling the RAF doctors. When he developed symptoms of diabetes (raging thirst, passing water, losing weight, lack of energy and compulsive eating), he recognized what they were from the symptoms his son had shown before being diagnosed with type 1 diabetes, so he went to a civilian doctor and managed his diabetes in private. This was a major undertaking. There were so many things he had to keep quiet from his colleagues—testing blood sugars, injecting insulin, eating snacks to avoid going low. What if he was in a meeting and went low? What if the RAF ever found out? It is an amazing story.

Mike and his son, Will, were organizing an inspirational expedition to the South Pole later that year. Our projects had much in common. We were aiming to raise awareness of diabetes, raise funds for diabetes research and to demonstrate that clinical conditions such as diabetes need not limit the scope of anyone's ambitions and accomplishments.

During the visit, I remembered a great joke we'd played on Mike 15 years earlier. Every couple of months the officers mess or squadron had a formal *dining in,* a feast with plenty of beer, wine and port, and plenty of fun and frivolity. At one of these, a rather destructive competition had been arranged to see which squadron could smash up a gambling (one-armed bandit) machine first! A cautionary instruction had been sent out by Wing Commander Cross to "Leave the mess piano alone!" Ha! It was a red cape to a bull. Our squadron found a cheap piano for $100 and substituted it for the real mess piano. While the gambling machines were being smashed up (and burned) that night in the mess car park, a shrill cry went out "GET THE MESS PIANO!" I've never seen a more energetic Wing Commander than Mike Cross desperately trying to pull people off the piano. It was a gallant effort, but an effort it remained. Sheer numbers prevailed, and the piano was duly smashed and burned. Mike was hopping mad. He was soon told the news, however, that the real mess piano was still "alive and well" and stored safely in a cupboard. Fortunately (for us) he saw the funny side.

I remember that Mike rang me soon after I was diagnosed. He explained his son's diabetes, sounding sympathetic and giving encouraging advice. I thought it was a very decent gesture at the time. Little did I know that he was speaking from experience, and that, in fact, he was empathizing. Of course at the time, he was not ready to let it be known. Mike informed the RAF authorities and went public (or as he says "came out") about his type 1 diabetes after he retired and when he committed to his son's South Pole expedition and its aims.

I felt mixed and strong emotions as I took off from Cranwell and returned to London. This had been a visit to my former life that had been so fulfilling, and that was cut off in its prime due to diabetes. What could have been I'll never know. I most likely never would have lived in Thailand. I certainly wouldn't have been flying a Baron around the world.

Malta—Keeping Diabetes Quiet

The flight to Malta from Cannes in southern France was full of anticipation. This was venturing over the Mediterranean Sea, a historic part of the world and extremely popular with the British seeking warm destinations—myself

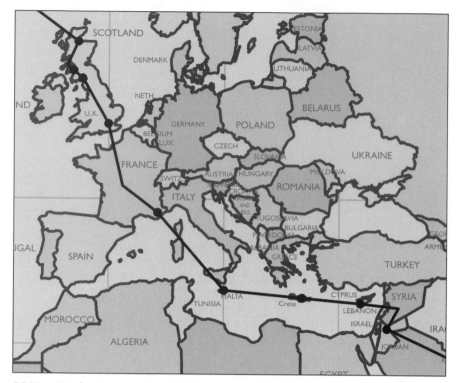

U.K. – Mediterranean Sea – Jordan

included. During our takeoff from Cannes, a sharp wind tumbled down from nearby mountains, resulting in a bumpy climb to cruising height. Further out to sea and as the air calmed, we could see the island of Corsica on the horizon, followed by Sardinia on our southward track. Three hours later Malta gradually appeared in hazy conditions, its sandstone cliffs rising high out of the sea with the sandstone brick buildings blending into the rocky landscape.

Malta has a turbulent and fascinating history. In 1565 the Turks orchestrated the four-month siege of Malta that resulted in more than 30,000 deaths including the slaying of half the Knights of Malta (about 350 men) and 8,000 soldiers before a Spanish army relieved the capital city of Valetta. After widespread destruction, Valetta had to be rebuilt, the result of which you see today: city walls rising sheer out of pearl-blue harbor waters, narrow streets framed by 400-year-old buildings, ornate doorways and windows, all contributing to the historic atmosphere. Valetta was under siege again in World War II when the Germans repeatedly bombed the island. This time it was the British who repelled the tenacious attacks.

On the first day in Malta, I took a slow bus winding around the eastern coastline toward Valetta, lapping up views of the harbor and the city in the background. I explored Valetta, absorbing the atmosphere while making my way to the tiny part-time office of Malta's Diabetes Association.

It was here I learned that Malta has made present-day history in the world of diabetes. Of Malta's total population (about 400,000 people), more than 10% have been diagnosed with diabetes. This is a terribly high number when compared to the U.S. at 5.7% and the U.K. at 3.8%, and one that puts great pressure on the healthcare system. Genetic susceptibility is believed to be responsible, since close family structures—cousins often marry cousins—are common, but a changing diet to more processed and fatty foods and resulting obesity is also believed to play a part.

I learned about negative perceptions of diabetes in outlying parts of Malta. Stigma came along with the assumption that all people with diabetes are sick and unhealthy. As a result, people sometimes tried to keep their diabetes quiet from members of their community, often making their medical condition tougher to accept and to control. The Diabetes Association is working hard to educate the island community about diabetes, to alleviate negative perceptions and to show how to prevent or delay the onset of type 2 diabetes with a healthy diet and regular exercise. The Association is also kept busy offering free blood glucose tests and reduced price test strips once a week at their office in Valetta.

A Sumptuous Feast

In Iraklion on the island of Crete, I met jovial Dr. Nikolas Kefalogiannis, vice president of the Hellenic Diabetologist Association. He treated me to a huge dinner of local goat and rabbit in a cozy local restaurant. His good friend, George Mavrantonakis, advisor to the President and CEO of Olympic Airways, was also there, eating with gusto. I was amused that the doctor kept pushing beers my way, followed by red wine and finally some very strong shots of Ouzo (the local drink)—just what the doctor should order for someone with diabetes! It was fun to sample local foods, beverages and, of course, the famous Greek hospitality.

Dr. Nikolas is a well-known diabetologist in Crete. One of his patients was an 82-year-old man who had lived with type 1 diabetes for 49 years. Despite being diagnosed when the method of checking blood sugar was testing urine (an inaccurate method no longer used) and when the average lifespan for a person with type 1 was much shorter than now, this man had enjoyed a healthy life and avoided any end-organ complications, such as kidney or eye disease. He was a retired farmer living in the mountains, a testament to the true benefits of regular exercise and eating a healthy local diet.

Fighter Jets

While researching Diabetes World Flight, I learned that fighter jets occasionally intercepted light aircraft in the Middle East, even when they were flying along recognized airways. Invariably, the jet pilots were just confirming who you were before peeling away and leaving you alone. Just in case this happened, before departing Cyprus for Jordan, I stowed a tiny camera by my blood glucose meter, in the hope of taking a surreptitious photograph.

As we approached the Lebanese coast from Cyprus, there were white contrails of fast jets in a racetrack pattern high above our airway and projected flight path ahead. Suddenly Beirut ATC warned, "November Three Zero Tango Bravo, you have four unidentified aircraft at 2 o'clock and 14 miles." This was odd. If aircraft were flying in Beirut's controlled airspace, ATC should know who they were. As we passed under the contrails, I looked up and saw four silver specks far above, fighter jets departing to the south toward Israeli airspace. So who were they? The following week we were chatting with some United Nations staff in Jordan, and they explained that Israeli jets had been flying over Lebanon, deliberately busting their airspace. This is exactly what we had seen.

The rest of the flight to Jordan was fascinating, and I used my tiny camera for some aerial photos. A direct route to Jordan from Cyprus would have been straight over Israel. However, Arab countries do not permit planes to enter from Israeli airspace. We had to dogleg east over Lebanon and into Syria before turning southwest to Jordan. We passed by Tripoli, climbed over Mt. Lebanon, and crossed over Bekka Valley and Syria's desert landscape. Descending straight into Queen Ahlia International Airport, we saw hundreds of Amman's rectangular and tightly packed houses in the background, illuminated by hazy sunshine. I was full of anticipation, this being my first visit to the Middle East.

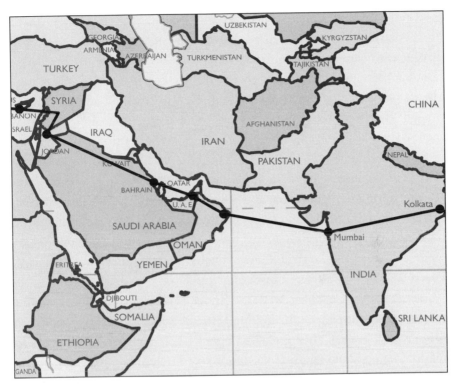

The Middle East – India

The Middle East

Evidence of tension in the Middle East was plain to see. In Jordan's capital city, Amman, an American diplomat had been shot and killed outside his house. The most direct airway from Jordan to Bahrain, which ran close to the Iraqi border, had been closed. At Bahrain Airport, there were several American military helicopters and transport planes parked beside us. I asked my clearance agent if any light aircraft passing through the Middle East had been experiencing problems. His answer was no, but he would let me know if he became aware of any.

As it turned out, the people I met in the Middle East were friendly and helpful. Arab people are encouraged to give up to 10% of their salary to charity, and perhaps the fundraising status of DWF helped. I was also passing through the more pro-western states of Jordan, Bahrain, United Arab Emirates and Oman. On arriving in Jordan, we were met and hosted by Cassie, a London friend now working with the United Nations. She seemed pretty relaxed about living in Amman as a Westerner.

A rather interesting moment occurred in Jordan, however. On the way to dinner one evening, we encountered a traffic jam on a narrow road. A car had broken down and its three Jordanian occupants, attired in white robes, were standing right in the middle of the road, blocking it unnecessarily. Cassie revved her jeep and accelerated. Their eyes widened in disbelief. They thought they were about to be run over by a Western female! They threw themselves to the side, and as we accelerated away, a few stones rained down on the back door.

It was fascinating to be in Jordan as Ramadan began. No eating was allowed during daylight hours, and while Westerners may be excused from this rule, it would be disrespectful to eat or drink in public. One evening, two on-duty policemen quietly squatted beside their car at the road edge, eating while contemplating a vivid sunset. Theirs was the only car to be seen. Everybody else was inside, eating a huge meal.

Restaurants offered huge feasts for dinner. Twice I gorged myself, topping up generously with fast-acting insulin. I was careful to avoid eating too much carbohydrate but still my sugars went high. (When the stomach is full, or distended, the body can release large amounts of insulin in anticipation, and to counteract this, the liver will release sugar into the bloodstream. Even though someone with diabetes will not deliver insulin from the pancreas automatically, the liver can still respond to a distended stomach and release sugar. This "Chinese dinner syndrome" can result in very high sugars after a huge meal even with zero carbohydrate.)

I wondered how people with insulin-dependent diabetes coped during Ramadan. The Jordanian diabetes association explained that the majority of people with diabetes are advised against fasting during Ramadan. According to the Qur'an (Koran), patients are exempted when it comes to Ramadan fasting.

Insulin Too Expensive

In Jordan, where the average monthly wage is 150 Jordan Dinars (approximately $225 U.S.), monthly insulin supplies take 20% of average wages for someone with insulin-dependent diabetes. This does not include the cost of blood sugar meters, test strips and syringes. Indeed, many Jordanian households find it extremely difficult to afford diabetes medication, and over the past few years, The Jordanian Society for the Care of Diabetes has assisted more than 1,150 people with insulin supplies but is running out of funds. Prior to 1998, fundraising was primarily done through a highly publicized Annual March, sponsored by a number of prominent companies. However, with tensions higher across the region, public gatherings or marches have been banned. Insulin donations are becoming increasingly difficult to finance.

Floating on the Dead Sea and Indiana Jones

Jordan is one of the most popular tourist destinations in the Middle East. It is easy to see why. On the second day, Cassie drove Ty and me into a deep valley heading toward the Dead Sea. Arid sandstone landscapes cast a spell as we gazed across at one of Israel's oldest biblical townships on the western shores of the Dead Sea. It was a cool autumn day in Amman, but as we descended into the valley, the temperature rose noticeably. Camels occasionally ambled across the road herded by Bedouin locals. The camels looked nonchalant and displeased at having to move, waving their heads, baring their yellow teeth and croaking loudly in defiance.

I was full of anticipation, conjuring up images of people floating incredibly high out of the water. We parked at an enclosed tourist spot and walked into a concrete shelter to change into swimming shorts. As we ventured down a gentle sandy slope, an overweight German tourist paraded at the water's edge in the briefest of swim suits, his stomach spilling over the top.

The water looked strange, translucent but hazy. The intense daytime heat in the below sea-level valley evaporates the water so rapidly that the amount of salt in solution has built up to 33% compared to 3% in the Mediterranean Sea. The salt makes the water much more dense, which results in the unnatural buoyancy of anything floating on it.

Cassie remained at the water's edge while we waded up to our waists and lowered ourselves in, careful not to splash water on our faces for fear of getting stinging salt in our eyes. I rolled onto my back and was amazed to find my arms and lower legs naturally extending into the air. Both Ty and I laughed out loud at this curious state of affairs. It was nearly impossible to swim because your hands and feet stick up above the water level. We sort of shuffled around in the water, making slow progress. Flipping over, we could force our hands down into the water and try a footless breaststroke. Our efforts were rewarded by intense pain when drops splashed on our faces. The salt solution stung the skin around our eyes, and we had to wade out and take time to recover. Later, a gentle breeze whipped up waves and tiny droplets flew right onto our faces. The result was the same—intense pain, refuge on the beach, resolution to be more careful and a return to the surreal experience. I could have stayed for hours.

At the water's edge, locals were selling medicinal mud, basically clay scooped up from the bottom. We joined in the ritual of smearing it all over and allowing the water to absorb or melt it away. The German traveler looked particularly amusing covered in generous dollops of mud. He found us amusing, too.

The following day, Ty and I rented a car and drove four hours south to Petra. Ramadan had already begun, but my insulin injections required snacks and meals at certain times to avoid going low. Whenever I was eating, I was careful to keep the food out of sight.

We snaked our way down into the village of Petra and found a basic hotel near the entrance to the historic site. It was November and out of season—very few people were around. After throwing our luggage into our rooms, we entered the Petra complex. We walked for more than a mile down a narrow, winding *wadi* (ravine). I was thinking about how flash floods of water forced their way down this ravine, digging it deeper over thousands of years to reach its present form. On one side of the ravine floor, man-made channels had been dug to prevent further erosion. The ravine floor descended gradually; the mid-afternoon sunshine glinted off the red rock walls of the ravine and we could see deep blue sky above us.

We came into an open area where elaborate buildings and tombs with grand facades were hewn into the sheer cliffs that rose several hundred feet up. Right in front of us was the most spectacular building in Petra, the Treasury Building. You would recognize it as the place where Indiana Jones (Harrison Ford) and his father (Sean Connery, my fellow Scotsman) came to find the Holy Grail in the third film in the *Indiana Jones* trilogy. By coincidence, it was the set for another film that day! I could imagine Jones dashing into the building and gallantly defeating the enemy. In front of us, however, were a couple of unkempt horses for tourists to hire, and a quietly disorganized film crew. It was strange. Silent structures extended on down the walls of the ravine. People had painstakingly chiseled these facades out of rock centuries ago, creating a city at the confluence of ancient trading routes.

Stigma and Misunderstanding

In Oman, I spoke for 10 minutes at a press conference held in the Muscat Sheraton Hotel, outlining Diabetes World Flight, and the point that people with diabetes can control their diabetes and lead normal lives. At the end of the talk, a respected journalist jumped up and said "Mr. Cairns. You look fit and healthy, and yet you have diabetes. Can you please explain yourself?" He clearly assumed that *all* people with diabetes were unfit and unhealthy. And he had the power to influence public opinion via his national newspaper articles. Part of me was taken aback at his question and underlying assumption. The other part was pleased to explain that, yes, people can have problems managing diabetes, but there are people who can control it well and indeed, do anything they put their mind to.

I was curious to see what this journalist would write for the following day's paper. The title was *Diabetic Patient Flies Around the World*. It conjured up an image of me being wheeled out to my plane on a hospital trolley attached to an intravenous drip! While it had been a tremendous opportunity for me to outline what *can* be done with diabetes, I have a feeling that this journalist's negative perception prevailed.

It's frustrating to encounter negative perceptions and attitudes and to know that they can lead to discrimination against people with diabetes. It's not really anybody's fault. Discrimination is often based on ignorance and fear. We have to work hard to improve the public's knowledge about and their perceptions of diabetes.

India

Mumbai, formerly known as Bombay, on the west coast of India was my first stop after the Middle East. This city is a fascinating mix of modern-day business, old colonial grandeur, crowded roads and abject poverty. Congested streets provide a cacophony of horn-blaring auto-rickshaws, motorbikes, cars, 1960s-style taxis, buses and lorries belching thick blue fumes, all vying aggressively for the fastest way through.

When I arrived in Mumbai after a six-hour flight from Oman, I had to park the plane at a remote unlit spot, and the plane was surrounded by four armed guards. While commercial jets screamed on takeoff nearby, the customs officer, Mr. I. H. Kate, searched inside the plane. He then asked me what Diabetes World Flight was all about. I was a bit worried about this questioning by a stern official. However, when I had explained the purpose of the flight, he exclaimed that he had type 2 diabetes. He couldn't afford his own blood glucose meter and test strips and only tested his sugar once a month when he visited his doctor for medication. He asked if I could test his sugar. I dug out a meter and test strip, inserted a clean lancet and checked his blood sugar on the spot. His reading was 112 mg/dl—normal. Mr. I. H. Kate, Customs Officer, suddenly became a good friend.

Many people in India, and other developing countries, cannot afford to buy a blood glucose meter and test strips, and they test only once a month at regular visits to the doctor or healthcare center. It's a far cry from the daily checks we can do in the West.

Mumbai is India's financial center and boasts some of the most expensive office space anywhere in the world. It also houses more than 16 million inhabitants, many of whom have migrated from rural India. Thousands of people live in fragile linen and corrugated iron shelters beside busy roads and railways. During the day, scantily clad children play by the roads, while in the evening people sleep on the pavements. At traffic lights, people came up to the taxi and begged for money. Many had open sores on their skin. As I wound down a window to give a few rupees, a girl thrust her hand into the car and grabbed all the money I had in my palm. It was distressing to see such desperate poverty.

On the first day, I caught a train to the southern part of Mumbai. I joined dozens of people hanging out of open doorways, warm air blowing against my face while I watched the city roll by. After exiting a crowded station, I made my way to a boat quay where I could take a short boat cruise on the harbor. Before I boarded the boat, a small girl, perhaps 8 years old, tugged at my arm and insisted in broken English that I pay for her to get on the boat. I really didn't want to, but she was a forceful little character. I walked back to the counter and paid for another ticket. She stood on the open deck and looked around at the harbor and city skyline. I chatted for a while with this independent little girl. She lived in a church refuge with her mother and baby brother. There was no mention of her father. On returning to the quay, she asked me if I would buy her some rice and baby food. She didn't want money, as she was too young to shop by herself. We walked to a corner shop by the quay, and I bought her enough rice for a month and baby food for three months. When other children saw me do this, they ran up, tugging sharply at my sleeve and begging for the same. Again, such desperation was distressing.

I felt glad that I could help this girl as I took a taxi back to the hotel. What an amazing contrast between such abject poverty and the luxury of the Airport Sheraton Hotel. The Sheraton was like a palace, a refuge from the onslaught of every day Mumbai life.

On the second day, I was distinctly ill, most likely from a yogurt eaten at breakfast. It's easy to fall sick while traveling in India, and I should have been more vigilant, particularly with dairy products.

I couldn't eat anything solid for two days, apart from a small apple, so I drank orange juice. (I also confess to having a small beer on the second day after meeting Ty by chance at the happy-hour bar.) I tested my blood sugars often. To my surprise, my blood sugar control was extremely good, hovering around 70 mg/dl almost all the time. Sugars can go high when one is ill, requiring more insulin. However, I was hardly eating anything. When I saw my sugars trending lower, I reduced my insulin a little to allow for the decreased carbohydrate intake. Fortunately this seemed to work well.

On the third day, I started to feel better. It was an enormous relief, in more ways than one. I had been worried about flying with diarrhea—you can imagine the nightmare if "caught short" mid-air.

The Impact of Urban Migration

In Mumbai, I met Dr. Sathe, the Secretary of the Indian Diabetes Association, at Raheja Hospital. Mumbai's poverty was shocking, and I was intrigued to find out how people coped with their diabetes. In developing countries, migration to the cities from rural areas is common, because people are attracted by hopes of higher earnings and a better standard of living. But with more money comes a change in diet away from fresh whole foods and a change in work from physical to sedentary work. Dr. Sathe described the result of urban migration as "the higher the affluence, the higher the incidence" of diabetes. In rural India, where diet and lifestyle have changed little over hundreds of years, the incidence of diabetes was less than 2% of the population. Urban areas, however, with their greater relative affluence, richer diets and more sedentary lifestyle show *triple* the incidence at 6%. And the numbers are rising.

Dr. Sathe believes that changed diet is the major reason for the difference between rural and urban incidence. He mentioned that India is leading research into how the balance of polyunsaturated fats (omega-6 and omega-3 fatty acids) has changed in people's diets over the years, and its connection with the increasing incidence of urban diabetes. There is much more omega-6 than omega-3 fat because vegetable and seed oils are replacing fats found in fenugreek, ghee, coconut and marine fish oils. A key phrase used by the diabetes association of India was "Treatment is not in the hospital but in the kitchen," in hopes of persuading people to eat more omega-3 fats. Omega-3 fats are found in olive oil, canola oil, flax seed oil, seeds such as ground flax seeds and sunflower seeds, and cold-adapted green plants. Animals cannot make their own omega-3 fats, so they must eat them. Some fish do contain omega-3 fats, but it is because they eat the tiny green plants in the cold water, or they eat the littler fish that eat those plants.

In Bangkok, Thailand, I took a long-tailed boat up the Chao Praya River, one of the most colorful and fascinating parts of the city. Diminutive but powerful tugboats pulled heavy barge convoys. Streamlined river buses forged along, stopping briefly at pontoon jetties where passengers jumped off precariously.

I leapt off my own boat near Siriraj Hospital where I met Professor Sunthorn Tanhanand, the President of the Thailand Diabetes Association. Thailand had seen a sharp increase in numbers of people with diabetes over the past three decades during which migration to cities has occurred with the expected lifestyle and diet changes. In 1965, less than 2.5% of the population had diabetes. By 2000, this had increased to 4.8%. A survey of people over 35 years old in 2001–2002 showed 9.6% with diabetes, an ominously high figure. It was fascinating to find that the numbers in the cities was triple the rural incidence, exactly the same result we saw in India.

An Amazing Coincidence

While in Jordan, I had been chatting with Cassie, our host, about my ex-wife, Chrissy. We had not been in touch for several years, and I thought that she was living in Sydney with her husband and child. Logging onto email later that day, I was astonished to find one from Chrissy, titled *Hello Stranger*. After the initial shock of the coincidence, I was delighted to hear from her. She had recently moved to Singapore and was now working with Edelman. Amazingly,

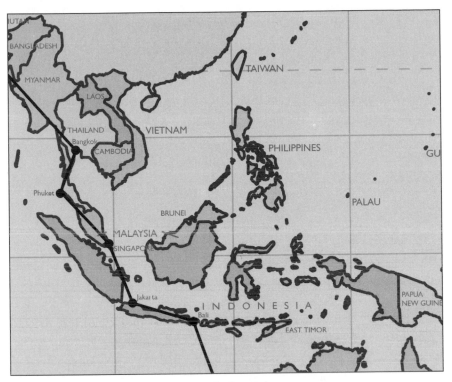

The Far East (Thailand, Singapore, Indonesia)

one of her clients was Accu-Chek, which was one of the companies making donations to my research fundraising effort. She asked if I would be willing to join a press conference when passing through Singapore and say a few words.

I was delighted at the prospect of working together. It was quite a thought though. We hadn't been in touch for at least three years and hadn't seen each other for nine years. It would be a strange experience.

As soon as I landed in Singapore, I rushed to a meeting that Chrissy was hosting. I had been looking forward to seeing her for the past month, and it was a pleasure to see her. We couldn't chat, however, because she had to leave for another meeting.

The next day I was due to talk at the press conference, and Chrissy was the master of ceremonies. It was difficult not to pinch myself as Chrissy introduced the speakers. It was as though I had gone back 10 years. She looked almost exactly the same, except for longer hair that suited her well. We both had a few more lines and, of course, a couple of gray hairs. While it seemed strange, it felt good to meet again. During the preliminary stages of the press conference, we sought each other out to have a quick chat in between media interviews and hosting. Later that day we met up for drinks.

It's difficult to catch up on nine years in 60 minutes. But we managed a lot. Chrissy had re-married and had two young children. The rest of her family was well in Australia. She had an excellent career in Singapore. She seemed fulfilled and happy. There's no doubt I came away with many thoughts and emotions whizzing around my head. I will always appreciate Chrissy's help for Diabetes World Flight while in Singapore. It was a major highlight of the whole project.

Bomb Zone

Bali is a stunning Indonesian tropical island with beautiful beaches and huge surf rolling in from the Indian Ocean. It normally has a vibrant tourist trade and is particularly popular among young Australians. One month before I passed through Bali, however, a terrorist bomb had exploded outside the Sari Club in Kuta, killing more than 150 people. Kuta, normally a bustling area, was now deserted.

It was sobering to talk with some locals at a bar near the flattened Sari Club. The bomb-blast death toll was believed to be higher than the official number. It was thought that several local people were pushing drugs outside the bar, and a number of "working girls" were also nearby when the bomb went off. Allegedly the authorities did not include these people in the death toll. Many were never identified.

The aftermath of this appalling explosion was only too evident. Tourist numbers were down by 85%. As many as 50% of local hotel employees had been laid off, some smaller hotels had closed, restaurants were empty and in the evenings, several normally popular bar and nightclub areas were totally deserted. Many tourist-related companies were going bust.

While we were watching a beautiful sunset from Kuta Beach, a beach vendor in his mid-thirties, came up to me and energetically persuaded me to buy a silk beach rug at a fraction of the normal price. I only had two thirds of the money he asked for, but he accepted anyway. He desperately needed the cash to survive. We agreed to meet at 6 p.m. the following evening when I would pay him the remainder. However, he didn't turn up the next day. I felt very sorry for this guy.

It was a tragic, desperate situation. Not only had 150 people been killed the previous month, but local people had been terribly affected by the loss of their livelihood. I wondered whether the terrorists, Muslim activists, had thought about the impact on the locals, their fellow citizens.

Shortage of Doctors

In Bali, I took a taxi to the peaceful Salang Hospital where I learned some sobering statistics from Dr. Dwi Sutenagara, the President of the Indonesian Diabetes Association. Indonesia is the most populous Muslim country in the world with 220 million inhabitants. Somewhere between 6 and 10 million people have diabetes. To help these millions who are spread over literally hundreds of islands, there were only 50 diabetes specialist doctors and 1,000 diabetes educators.

Being able to afford medication is also an issue. There is no government healthcare system, and many find it difficult to afford insulin and blood pressure medication for people with type 2 diabetes and high blood pressure—a truly dangerous combination. The Indonesian minimum monthly wage is 300,000 Rupiah (approximately $35 U.S.) and monthly insulin costs totaled 100,000 Rupiah (RP), with a blood glucose meter alone costing 1 million RP. Families tried to help out, but with costs taking up to one third of a household's income, what people could buy was seriously limited. Many doctors' surgeries donate medicine, but people cannot rely on this indefinitely.

Blood testing for many was just too expensive. People relied on visiting a clinic or surgery twice a month for blood tests. Such frequency for those with type 1 diabetes is a fraction of the recommended four tests a day, and this has an impact on blood sugar control and, consequently, long-term health. Just as it is in Jordan, this is a desperate situation, and the recent tsunami damage has surely worsened conditions for those with diabetes.

Shark Bay

December 21 was our first day in Australia and the first opportunity since the U.K. to fly VFR (visual flight rules) as opposed to IFR (instrument flight rules). The day before I had collected the required maps and airport facility handbooks from Port Hedland Airport. It was time for some fun flying.

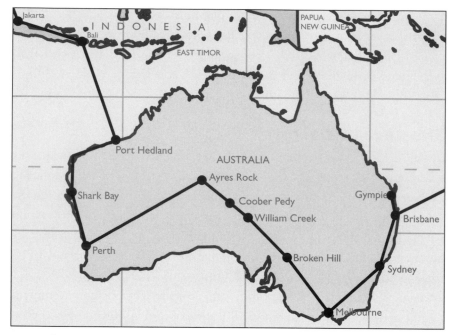

Around Australia

Australia is famous for its stunning coral reefs and aquatic life, and today's destination was Shark Bay, well-known for its teeming marine life. After we filled up with gas donated by Air BP, it was incredibly refreshing to have the freedom of VFR flying. We didn't have to talk to Air Traffic Control, unless flying near or over a controlled airfield.

The plan was to follow the coast at low-level for 500 miles west and then south to Carnarvon to refuel and then make a short hop to Shark Bay. West of Port Hedland we flew over mangroves and endless miles of unspoiled and rarely visited beaches. We flew for scores of miles without seeing anyone or any buildings. One beach had three hapless looking kangaroos munching away on scraggly vegetation. Given Australia's prevailing drought conditions, it was difficult to see how they could survive.

North of Carnarvon I flew low over Lake MacLeod, a large salt-pan which can only be described as extremely inhospitable land. It was hot in the cockpit at low level. After refueling at Carnarvon, it was a short hop of just 60 miles to Shark Bay.

Before reaching Shark Bay Airport, I flew low and slow (100 knots) over the beaches around Monkey Mia Dolphin Resort. People go there to see the wild dolphins feed at the water's edge under the watchful eyes of park rangers. The water was a shimmering azure blue and crystal clear from above. I was amazed to see two tiger sharks swimming in shallow water. (I shouldn't have been that amazed—it's called Shark Bay for a reason.) We spotted several dolphins cruising in the shallows and then dozens upon dozens of manta rays swimming in formation. These were captivating sights, and it took considerable will power to turn the Baron away and land at the nearby airport.

On the last run along the Monkey Mia Dolphin Resort, we spotted a large tiger shark just 150 yards off the beach. This is where we were staying that night, so I made a mental note not to swim alone or very far out (or to make sure there was someone swimming further out than me). Tiger sharks can be indiscriminate about feeding, and I remember watching a documentary on Shark Bay that described a ferocious attack on an Aboriginal person many years ago. According to the airport bus driver, though, food supply was plentiful for the sharks, including old or ill dugongs and dolphins. According to local marine research, 70% of the dolphin community showed signs of shark bites. In the resort's 30-year history, nobody had ever been attacked. One hopes this will remain the case.

Sir John The Diabetic Dog

While I was in Bangkok, I met the Reverend Dr. Richard Martin of Gympie, Australia, who invited me to fly up from Brisbane (in Australia) to meet the Gympie Diabetes Support Group. On Saturday, 10 January, I departed Archerfield Airport on a sunny day and flew north over rolling countryside and semi-tropical vegetation. Halfway there, I wheeled around the Glass House Mountains named by explorer James Cook, who likened the glistening rock faces to glass houses. These sheer volcanic cones rise vertically out of the plains, creating quite a surreal atmosphere.

Gympie Airfield is a few miles outside the town, bang in the middle of the countryside. I wondered if kangaroos could be hopping around the runway. *Hmmm, time for a low pass to find out!* From 20 feet and 175 knots, the runway looked clear. Pulling up sharply, I reduced power and turned to join the downwind leg allowing the Baron to climb to 800 feet above the runway and settle at 120 knots, with the undercarriage and approach flaps lowered. There's no doubt that a low pass is a great way to check that the runway is clear of kangaroos!

A reception of more than 40 people from the Gympie Diabetes Support Group and Gympie Airsports Club awaited us. We spent a tremendous couple of hours, with a classic Aussie BBQ, chatting with various folk and giving a quick presentation on DWF.

I met Angus and Gem Hutton, owners of a wonderful dog named Sir Joh (pronounced "Joe"), a fine cross between a Golden Labrador and Beagle, with the best of both temperaments. Seven years earlier, Angus and Gem noticed Sir Joh losing weight—16 pounds in all. He became too weak to walk, and suspecting some kind of poisoning, Angus and Gem took him to the vet. A blood test showed a sugar level of 38 mmol/l or 684 mg/dl. He had type 1 diabetes. Ten minutes after an insulin injection, Sir Joh's tail wagged for the first time in ages.

Angus and Gem learned all they could about canine diabetes and embarked on a disciplined management of Sir Joh's diabetes. In all respects, they set a great example of dedicated and conscientious care, much like parents looking after a child. Angus and Gem injected Sir Joh with insulin each day, tested his blood sugar regularly, fed him two balanced meals a day and took him for regular exercise. Sir Joh was a friendly and spirited dog, and Angus and Gem derived great pleasure from his good health and companionship. This was the first time I had met an animal with diabetes. Angus, Gem and Sir Joh's active membership in the local diabetes support group is a great testament to the Australian spirit.

Keeping the Safety Pilot

One of the challenges during DWF was keeping my second safety pilot, Ty, who joined me in Scotland. It started with a remarkable coincidence in Malta. One morning in our small hotel, I found Ty looking quite distressed. He told me that his fiancée, Maria, had just been admitted to hospital in Miami with very high blood pressure. While in hospital, she had been diagnosed with type 2 diabetes.

"What! Type 2 diabetes!" I exclaimed. Although my diabetes is type 1, most of the information being posted on my website diary was relevant to type 2. It seemed a cruel irony. Maria was a classic candidate for type 2 diabetes. She was 51 years old, Hispanic (with higher genetic risk of being diagnosed) and had put on weight over the past few years. Ty was understandably upset. I suggested he go back to Florida for 10 days to be with her, but he said no, that he would remain "for the cause." With Maria's diabetes, he now felt that "the cause" was even more meaningful. I was grateful. However, Ty found DWF very difficult from this point on. Understandably, he desperately missed Maria and wanted to be with her.

Ty had been working out well. After the first few flights, he seemed to settle into the non-active safety pilot role well. He appeared happy to do his own thing at each destination while I was busy with meetings and media. He was putting his time to good use by learning Spanish in his hotel room. Maria was from Puerto Rico, and he wanted to be fluent by the time he saw her again in three months.

When we reached Dubai two weeks later and stayed with Colin and Pauline Bodie, old RAF friends, Ty mentioned how difficult he was finding the trip and doubted whether he could last the remaining three months. I suggested that he go back to Florida to see Maria while the plane had its 100-hour check in Thailand. This would give him a good 10 days at home. He loved the idea, and this is exactly what he did.

While he was in Florida, however, I wondered if he would come back. He did come back and was in great form. Maria was feeling much better, having lost 26 pounds, reduced her blood pressure and, as a result of both, had brought her type 2 diabetes symptoms under control. Ty was sincerely appreciative for having had the opportunity to go back. However, by the time we landed in Australia, 12 days later, I sensed that Ty was still finding it difficult being away from Maria. Not only that, he seemed distressed at the flies when we landed in Port Hedland, Australia. Not a good omen—there are zillions of aggressive flies in Australia. (You cannot imagine what it's like if you haven't been there.) And Ty had developed an intestinal illness to add to his discomfort.

We stayed with old University friends of mine in Perth, and on Christmas Day, Kev and Sandra served a very enjoyable celebratory breakfast. I gave Ty an Icubra hat with corks dangling off the edges. These corks are designed to swing around when you move your head, keeping away the flies. Ty was genuinely thankful. Later that morning, we took off for a six-hour flight to Uluru, also known as Ayres Rock—a sacred place for the Aboriginal people of Australia. The next two days we were in Ayres Rock Resort, and it was clear that Ty was still washed out from his illness. I checked if he was okay for the onward flights.

Two days after Ayres Rock, we flew into William Creek, an extremely, hot, dusty and remote outback spot, with just a few corrugated iron-roofed huts and one tin-roofed hotel that sits beside the dirt runway. When we opened the aircraft door, the flies were utterly appalling. Thousands of them descended onto the plane, buzzing around our heads and getting into our eyes, mouth, ears and noses. They were disgusting. Ty was clearly distressed, so I told him to make a dash for the hotel while I locked up the plane. I caught a glimpse of Ty as he trotted falteringly, waving his arms and stopping every few yards to swipe at the flies. I followed with a vision in my mind of Benny Hill chasing semi-naked women, arms-a-waving—we were running the same way but arms-a-waving at thousands of pesky flies.

There's no doubt that the William Creek flies were quite a traumatizing experience. When I entered the pub, intensely relieved to escape the onslaught, Ty was perched on a stool at the far end, red-faced and staring. He shouted, "I will not tolerate this. We will not land anywhere like this again!" In the heat of the moment, he turned to the barman and said, "How can you *live* here?"

The barman looked at Ty and with classic Ozzie dryness said, "I lease the hotel, mate."

While the flies buzzed outside, I lapped up the ambiance of this true outback pub. The walls were covered with message-adorned shirts plus hundreds of student matriculation and ID cards, "donated" by travelers after many a boozy night. I could imagine people waking up the following morning with a stinking hangover, wondering where their ID cards were. John Sheedy, the hotel leaseholder, chatted amiably with us. He had thrown in his long-term job in cosmopolitan Melbourne and moved to this settlement totaling seven full-time inhabitants, bang in the middle of Australia's desert. A greater contrast to his former life you just couldn't imagine.

As we flew away later that day, I apologized, "I'm sorry you're finding this so hard with the flies." What followed was Ty's forthright expression of his thoughts, particularly of the hideous flies. It was a tense few minutes inside the cockpit, but outside it was beautifully sunny and clear. We flew over Flinders Ranges and Lake Frome, and then descended to low-level flight over Lake Eyre and some picturesque creeks and scrub-covered hills to the north of Broken Hill. The air temperature was 40°C outside, over 110°F, and without any air conditioning, it was stifling in the cockpit. After a few minutes, I climbed back up into cooler air.

At higher altitude I pondered the day's events and discussion. Ty had been ill with a stomach bug for the past week and even though I had checked to be sure he was okay to fly each day, he was likely still suffering. Moreover, I had definitely misjudged how bad the flies were for Ty since landing in Port Hedland. That night in Broken Hill (with noticeably fewer flies), we had another discussion over dinner. Ty was missing Maria bitterly, worrying about her health, and along with the environmental challenges was finding the trip quite an ordeal. He couldn't wait for it to finish, so he could get back to Maria.

Fortunately the extreme Australian outback conditions proved to be the only tense moment of our pilot-to-safety pilot relationship. A few days later we flew five separate legs between Melbourne and Sydney, taking 11 hours from start to finish. Ty was a real trouper. It was an excellent start, with Dr. Paul Zimmet, Helen Maxwell-Wright and Shirley Murray of the International Diabetes Institute in Melbourne coming out to see us off, along with a Channel 7 television crew, Ron Raab of Insulin for Life and three of my good old Bangkok friends, Hugh, Noirin and Liz. I first flew a five-minute circuit pattern at Morrabbin Airport, which Ty filmed using the Channel 7 (expensive!) camera. He then patiently waited at the next three destinations while I met with various people at a recently-opened flying school for the disabled in Cooma, an aviation doctor at Canberra's Australian Civil Aviation Safety Authority, and the manager of a ranch belonging to a two-time world flight pilot and Australian entrepreneur, Dick Smith. At the end of the day, I thanked Ty for the long day's work. I genuinely appreciated his patience and spirit. It was good to feel back to normal.

We had one more month of flying across the Pacific Ocean and would experience much together. There were frustrating but occasionally amusing airport admin difficulties to endure. We met appalling and potentially dangerous weather conditions at Christmas Island. Ty carried out his safety pilot duties with aplomb. On his final flight in Hawaii, Ty thanked me for the opportunity to fly around the world. I thanked him for sticking with Diabetes World Flight. I was truly grateful.

There was a perfect ending to Ty's safety pilot activities. Maria traveled to Hawaii to join him, and on February 5, 2003, they were married in

Honolulu. I felt happy and honored to be there. Maria was looking terrific. It was a simple, yet moving, ceremony by the sea with a minister and a photographer. Ty made a loving speech in Spanish. It was one of the best weddings I have been to, and I enjoy keeping in touch with Ty, following his progress in his new career.

Sydney from a Helicopter

My visit to Sydney proved to be a memorable few days. I met with a local Sydney diabetes support group and met a wonderful lady, Nancy Bird, who had been Australia's first female commercial pilot, flying biplanes around the outback with nothing more than basic maps and roads or tracks to find incredibly remote spots. Now in her mid 80s, she had tremendous spirit and enthusiasm for life.

I also met Dick Smith, a famous Australian businessman and highly respected pilot. He had flown two record-breaking flights around the world, once in a Bell helicopter (the first solo helicopter flight) and once via both poles in a Twin Otter airplane. He had also been the Chairman of the Australian Aviation Authority. A couple of people suggested I contact him, so I did, and much to my delight, he invited me around to his Sydney home for dinner.

Dick was well known for being a down-to-earth and decent individual, and this is exactly how he struck me. Dinner was replete with fascinating flying stories, and he showed great interest in the U.S. system for flying with diabetes. When I explained how it worked, Dick offered to help publish an article on it in the Australian Aircraft Owners and Pilot's Association magazine. I was very grateful.

I was also grateful for another reason, something quite unexpected. On meeting me at his doorstep, he immediately asked if I'd like to go flying. "Yes," was my answer, thinking we'd nip over to a hangar where he kept his helicopter or a plane. He took the stairs down to his basement, but this was not your average basement. Sitting on an electric trolley was a gleaming Bell helicopter. Dick flipped a switch and the "hangar" door opened while he maneuvered his helicopter-laden trolley out into an open garden area. We climbed in, Dick on the right hand seat as captain, and me on the left as passenger—the opposite way around from flying a fixed-wing aircraft. The jet engine whined into life, rotor blades accelerating above. I noticed how new everything looked—the instrument panel was polished and clean, without a scratch on it. My Baron was 33 years old and had lots of "character" by comparison. This was like sitting in the Hawk Jets I used to fly in the RAF, crisp and clean with an air of the latest technology. It was great.

Dick lifted the collective and the surrounding landscape suddenly came into view. Through the headphones lilted an *Enya* ballad as we accelerated over eucalyptus-tree-clad ridges and down toward the Pacific Ocean. It was a stunning way to see the suburbs of Sydney. Dick explained how he had helped establish routes for low-flying aircraft including helicopters, and we followed one of these to the coast and toward Sydney Harbor. Sydney is often described as one of the most beautiful cities you will ever find, and on this day, I agreed. We flew into the Harbor toward the white-winged Opera House and Sydney Harbor Bridge, the central business district skyline glistening in late afternoon sunshine. On the way back, Dick gave me the controls. We were in cruise mode so control-column inputs were the same as for a conventional aircraft. However, I kept moving the column slightly from side to side, trying to stop a mild oscillation. This seemed to make it worse, but Dick soon put me right. I had to keep the control column still to stop the oscillation. It definitely seemed like a smooth touch was required for helicopters (something no doubt I'd need to practice a lot).

New Caledonia

New Caledonia is French territory and a stunning set of tropical islands sitting 650 nautical miles to the northeast of Australia. It was our first stop in the Pacific Ocean. At Noumea, the capital city, a retired aviation authority official, Yannick Bonnace, kindly hosted us. Through Yannick, I met Dr. Jean Michel Tivollier, a nephrologist (kidney specialist), and he invited me to fly up to Koumac in the far north of the main island (La Grande Terre) to visit a renal unit run by Association pour la Prevention et la Traitement de L'Insuffisance Renale (ATIR).

Jean Michel has an enviable combination of medical work and pleasure. Once a week, he rents a Noumea Magenta Aero Club aircraft and flies to remote renal units where patients undergo dialysis. Well over 30% of these patients have diabetes, hence the invitation for me to visit.

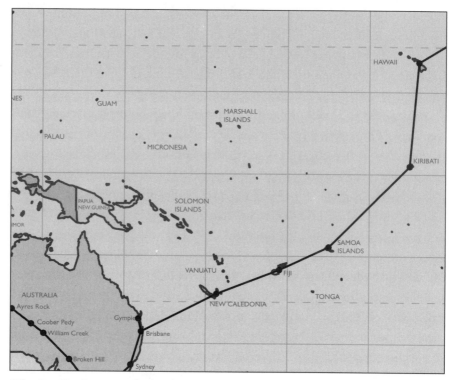

The Pacific Ocean and islands

On the morning of January 15th, Jean Michel took off in his single-engine Tobago (not surprisingly, a French plane), and we followed about half an hour later in N30TB. I had spent some time with Yannick, our host, the previous day, studying the local VFR maps and making sure that I was familiar with the required procedures. We were asked to delay our takeoff in the Baron to avoid a commercial flight going into an airport further along the coastline. They were concerned that our lack of French could lead to a potential communication problem in the air. No problem. We'd already had a nightmare with French accents when we flew into Magenta just three days earlier. I was happy to wait.

New Caledonia gained its name from James Cook in 1774, when from a distance, he saw similarity between the island's mountains and those of the Scottish Caledonian Highlands. Soon after taking off, we tracked the coastline northward. Azure blue lagoon waters were lined with fringing reefs, contrasting vividly against the green inland mountains. I mused a little on just how different this was from Scotland. This was tropical bliss, with sunny weather, coral reefs and inviting waters. *There ain't no tropical waters, tropical weather or fringing reefs around Scotland!* However, beautiful mountains there were, and from our aerial vantage I could see definite similarities.

Two-thirds into the flight we passed over Le Coeur de Voh, a perfect heart-shaped outline in natural vegetation. This beautiful sight is apparently famous. A French policewoman had described it the day before and was amazed I'd never heard of it. Approaching Koumac at the northwest end of La Grande Terre Island, 160 miles from Noumea, we flew around some extensive mountaintop open-cast nickel mines. New Caledonia's economy relies heavily on mining and metallurgy, with nickel mining and smelting accounting for the bulk of economic output and foreign earnings. The result of this is that some large mountaintops are stripped bare, the scars of which are visible from many miles away.

About five miles from Koumac, Jean Michel was on the radio to find out where I was. We were only two minutes apart—great timing. Both Ty and I visited the Koumac renal unit where there was an attractive French nurse with four patients undergoing dialysis, one of whom had type 2 diabetes. Jean Michel introduced me to each patient. They were all indigenous New Caledonians, subdued and contemplative, trying to relax while dialysis machines cleaned their blood. Most indigenous Pacific Island populations suffer higher than average genetic susceptibility to type 2 diabetes. Meanwhile, changing diets (more refined foods) were most likely responsible for increasing incidence of obesity, which in turn increased the numbers of type 2 diabetes alarmingly. I found this to be true all the way to Hawaii.

It was a sobering experience. I had not seen dialysis up close before, and it was a powerful motivator to continue to strive for good long-term diabetes control. So far I did not have any signs of diabetes complications. I wanted to keep it that way.

I was soon to learn, however, that these patients, in many respects were lucky. New Caledonia is one of only a few Pacific Island nations that have dialysis machines. There were no machines in Fiji, Samoa and Kiribati, the island nations I passed through next. In Fiji, where the average annual salary was $4,000, people were told to "Find $50,000 or die." The only option was to have a kidney transplant in Australia or New Zealand. At least in Samoa, people could benefit from peritoneal dialysis. The government would pay for people to travel to Australia or New Zealand where a catheter was inserted into the stomach wall. This would then be used to flush out the stomach cavity regularly back in Samoa. Apparently not everybody had this option, though. I was told that the government had to make choices based on budget constraints and the individual's status. One person suggested that it could sometimes be a political decision.

It was one of those times to reflect and realize how lucky we are in industrial nations, where healthcare is usually well developed and treatments such as dialysis are available. Cost could be an issue, but at least we have access to the treatments. The annual cost per person for dialysis in New Caledonia was $50,000. This figure was based on operating costs of dialysis three times a week per person, equipment depreciation, personnel requirements, and the cost for the renal unit's buildings. The New Caledonia government and health insurance covered these costs. In Fiji and Samoa, the government could not afford such expenses.

As we drove back to the remote airfield, I thought about flying in New Caledonia. It was refreshing to find such freedom in the skies. I didn't have to get permission to fly, nor did I have to file a flight plan. I could just take off and contact airports as we neared them. We were in French territory, effectively flying in European airspace—but on the opposite side of the world from Europe.

During the flight back to Noumea a couple of mating dragonflies buzzed through the plane to the front, hitching a ride unwittingly. As Ty wrestled with this loving pair, I couldn't help laughing to myself about an amusing spoof message I'd received on the website from friends Gillem and Jamie in Bangkok. It read:

> *justin.vention@ Homepage URL: http://www.slapiton.com*
> *Comments: Dear Mr. Cairns I have this morning perused your website with some interest and feel we at Justin Vention Ltd. have a product that may be very useful for you. Australian flies can be very irritating at this time of year, particularly in dusty, outback locations where kangaroo carcasses are often stored near runways for human fast food purposes. We have recently patented a highly secret product which was originally invented to keep sheep safe from isolated farmers. We have evidence, from quite considerable experimentation, that flies are in fact slightly less interested in sheep which use our product than are*

farmers, but both farmers and flies are usefully repelled. The sheep we used in our study were really very attractive you understand, so this may explain the farmers' relatively higher enthusiasm.....

After the wrestling finished (the dragonflies lost), we had a peaceful few moments flying by Mont Panie, the island's highest mountain, (5,341 feet), and seeing beautiful waterfalls cascading down sheer rock faces. Views of the blue lagoon waters and tiny sand-fringed tropical islands were stunning. I brushed by hillsides, dived down remote jungle-filled valleys, cruised over uninhabited highlands, and circled the tiny islands. We passed more nickel mining complexes on high ground, enormous areas of exposed earth and rock. Scars to the naked eye, they represented past and present economic survival to New Caledonia. Finally we followed a deep valley leading to the other side of La Grande Terre. Descending from the northwest, we saw Noumea basking in late afternoon sunlight, anticipating a vivid sunset.

This had been a tremendous day. It was fascinating to visit the renal unit, and how lucky we were to enjoy a rare opportunity to fly around one of the world's most beautiful tropical islands.

Genetics and Diabetes

In Australia and on the islands of the Pacific Ocean, genetics play a major role in the higher incidence of type 2 diabetes. Indigenous populations already have a higher genetic risk of developing diabetes. With the advent of changing diet, usually with more junk food or highly processed foods and a more sedentary lifestyle, type 2 numbers are going sky high. Another example: on Christmas Island (Kiritimati) in Kiribati, 10% of its 8,000 people have diabetes.

In Coober Pedy, bang in the middle of Australia, I met Roland Ruff, the local Nursing Unit Manager. Ruffy knew much about diabetes, having been forced to leave his career in Movement Control in the Australian Army when diagnosed with type 1 diabetes in his 20s. After changing to a nursing career, Ruffy spent 16 years as a Remote Area Nurse working in the outback, often with the Aboriginal people. While approximately 6% of the Australian population has diabetes, the incidence among Aboriginal people is estimated at

20%. The change from a hunter-gatherer lifestyle to a Western lifestyle with richer diet, plus alcohol abuse, has taken its toll over the decades.

In Fiji I met with Ashok Patel, an extremely hard-working and inspirational Indian man who held the Medal of the Order of Fiji (equivalent of the British MBE) for his service to the community, including the Fiji National Diabetic Foundation. Ashok explained that Fiji's diabetes incidence is estimated at 20% of the total population, a terribly high figure. A recent diabetes awareness campaign had carried out 10,000 blood sugar tests, resulting in the diagnosis of 3,000 people—30% of those tested. Fiji's population had seen a shift to a richer diet and more sedentary lifestyle over the last few decades, leading to greater incidence of obesity and, in turn, type 2 diabetes. Genes play a large part in this—Fiji's population is approximately 58% indigenous Fijians and 42% Indian, all with high genetic susceptibility to type 2 diabetes.

Wendy Sefo, Executive Director of the American Diabetes Association (ADA) Hawaii Chapter, explained that the incidence of diabetes in Hawaii is almost two percentage points higher than on the mainland U.S. One in four native Hawaiians over the age of 30 has type 2 diabetes. Again, Hawaii's indigenous population of Pacific Islanders is more susceptible to type 2 diabetes.

Lessons from Samoa

Samoa, in the middle of the Pacific Ocean, has an easy-going pace of life. Nobody's in a rush, and if you are in a hurry, people look at you with a quizzical expression.

On the first day I took an energetic hike up a steep hill and visited the grave of Robert Louis Stevenson, a fellow Scotsman and author of *Treasure Island*. I could see why he had lived here from 1890 until his death in 1894. He had suffered from tuberculosis, and Samoa's warm climate must have made his life easier compared to the chilly U.K. He lived in a beautiful house with lush grounds overlooking the Pacific Ocean.

On the second day, I met with Dr. Satu Viali, an energetic and enthusiastic consultant in sole charge of the nation's diabetes healthcare. It was an informative visit. A survey in 1978 showed the incidence of diabetes at 6% of the total population of Samoa, but a survey in 1991 revealed a shocking increase to 11.5%. This was a near doubling in just 13 years! Another survey in 2002 is likely to yield significantly higher figures. Increased incidence of type 2 diabetes has coincided with a developing economy with urban migration, sedentary jobs and lifestyle, mechanized transport (instead of walking) and richer diets leading to more obesity and in turn, more type 2 diabetes. There were only 20 cases of diagnosed type 1 diabetes in the whole of (Independent) Samoa. This is only 0.1% of people with diabetes and is one of the lowest ratios worldwide. It is normally 5–10% of a population.

Dr. Satu estimated that more than 75% of Samoan adults are overweight with probably 50% classified as obese. He explained how culture plays a part in type 2 diabetes. Older people generally "take it easy," and apart from young people playing rugby and soccer, exercise is unpopular. Samoa is a communal society where people enjoy visiting each other often. Formal visits include large offerings of food, and it is rude to refuse. People are likely to overeat, put weight on, and can develop diabetes more easily. If you already have type 2 diabetes, it is more difficult to control blood sugar levels. Trying to get people to change their eating habits (reduce carbohydrate) and increase the amount of exercise they do is extremely difficult.

On the last night in Samoa, I met with Afamasaga Toleafoa, the slim 57-year-old editor of the *Samoa Observer*, in Aggie Grey's Hotel. Afamasaga had been a career diplomat and had always been slim, fit and healthy. As he said, he "knew the benefits" of a healthy lifestyle. But being so slim, he was often approached by people his age saying, "You're a disgrace to our generation." Wow—try to change this societal approach to food, lifestyle and obesity! Dr. Satu has a lot of work to do; it's a good thing he is an energetic man.

Hairy Moments

During an around-the-world flight with 187 hours flying time over some of the most remote regions of the globe, it's not surprising to have a couple of "hairy" moments on the way. Picking up icing in sleet and snow in Canada was particularly unpleasant. Flying through an intense rainstorm in Indonesia, we saw such heavy rain and turbulence that part of the decal on the nose of the plane was stripped off.

Landing in truly appalling weather at Kiritimati (Christmas Island) in the remote Pacific territory of Kiribati was one of the most thought-provoking moments. The forecast for arrival had been good, but after eight hours of solid flying from Samoa, about 40 miles from the island we encountered intense rainstorms with cloud almost on the deck. As we approached, we couldn't contact the air traffic controller to obtain an accurate altimeter setting. It was beginning to get dark, and without an air traffic controller to switch the runway lights on, we were in big trouble if we couldn't make a successful instrument approach. The closest airfield to divert to was 500 miles away, also unmanned and unlit. We just *had* to get down safely before darkness fell.

I dialed in a conservative estimate for the altimeter pressure setting, erring so that if anything we would be slightly high. I also concentrated extremely hard to fly an accurate GPS instrument approach. We were in thick cloud and heavy rain, and I was worried that we wouldn't see the runway from the 400 feet minimum descent height. If not, I'd have to carry out a missed approach, climb away and set up for another approach. We probably had *just* enough time for one missed approach to land before total darkness. Indeed, time was very tight.

A couple of miles from the airport, there was a brief break in the clouds and I could just make out a gray line ahead—the runway. *Relief!* I immediately dived down and scraped in below the next bank of cloud. Once on the ground, with rain splattering the cockpit canopy, I took a deep breath and relaxed. From extreme concern, I now felt relief and exhilaration at finishing the flight this way—landing safely in potentially dangerous conditions.

As I parked the plane, a smiley-faced individual wearing only shorts and flip-flop sandals rode up on his motorbike and greeted us. Grinning, he leaned on the wing and exclaimed, "I was expecting you tomorrow!" He was the air traffic controller who had just heard us fly overhead and rode in from his near-by home. (This guy must have one of the best jobs around—he greets one weekly flight from Hawaii and spends the rest of his time fishing in a beautiful lagoon.) While offloading the plane, we had to dash in the rain over to a dilapidated wooden terminal building to deposit luggage. A local guy kindly gave us a lift in his pick-up truck to the island's one and only hotel. Suffice to say, Ty and I enjoyed a couple of beers that night to celebrate our safe arrival.

Shortage of Insulin

Kiritimati or Christmas Island is an extremely remote spot 1,200 miles south of Hawaii, just north of the equator. Oddly, flying eight hours from Samoa, we had crossed the International Dateline for the second time and landed at

Christmas 32 hours after our takeoff! There was neither a television nor a telephone in the hotel. The only form of communication was a radio transmitter/receiver used to speak with other islanders.

Beside the hotel were narrow sandy beaches where huge crabs scuttled away to hide under bushes as I approached. At the end of the day, I sat at the beach in showers of rain and marveled at the fact that in front of me was 4,000 miles of open water all the way to the Philippines. It really is remote.

Christmas Island is government-owned and run and is effectively a huge coconut plantation. The highest point on the island is 15 feet above sea level. A large lagoon teems with fish life and several American fishing enthusiasts were staying at the island's only hotel—basic but comfortable—on package holidays. One of the fishermen had a few beers on the second night and asked what we were doing if not fishing. After Ty explained the world flight, the fisherman shouted rather drunkenly, "It's nice to know you while you're still alive!" I laughed, but tucked this comment away—it was a bit too close for comfort.

On January 30th, I took the hotel minibus into London, the main settlement on Christmas Island, to meet Dr. Eritane Kamatie, District Medical Officer. He explained that Kiribati's government supplied all healthcare and medication, but the island had recently run out of rapid-acting insulin. Before running out he'd had to ration it. I thought about how distressing this would be—controlling your diabetes would be impossible. I was further shocked to learn that there were only two blood glucose meters for all the people with diabetes on Christmas Island and two nearby islands. TWO kits for 800 people?? This was incredible. Control as we know it would just not be possible. It was a desperate situation.

In turn, I was glad to tell Dr. Eritane that I was carrying insulin supplies for him, 11 blood glucose monitors and many test strips donated by Ron Raab of Insulin for Life in Melbourne. Dr. Kamatie is an elderly doctor, with wisps of silver hair lying across his scalp. He peered at me through thick glasses with a bewildered expression on his face. He couldn't quite believe that a Western guy had just pitched up out of nowhere carrying two large boxes of desperately needed insulin and glucose meter supplies. Once it registered, he seemed subdued yet deeply grateful, saying how he would be able to leave some blood glucose meters on the two nearby islands for his patients to use.

We had carried the two boxes in the plane from Melbourne, Australia, and at each stop before Christmas Island (New Caledonia, Fiji and Samoa), I had to "smuggle" the box containing insulin through customs. It was necessary to store this box in at least hotel-room air conditioning where it could remain below 30°C (90°F). If insulin had been left in the aircraft parked in blistering sunshine, the heat could have destroyed the potency before it reached the final destination.

This incident made me think how lucky we are in the West to have *access* to medication. I guess we can take our health services for granted all too easily, complaining when things change or are not convenient. This is understandable. But just think about running out of insulin supplies! Or having to share one of two blood glucose meters with 800 other people with diabetes. It's quite unimaginable. However, this is what people on Christmas Island, and indeed, other countries around the world, have to live with.

The Flight from Christmas

The day before the flight from Christmas Island to Hawaii, I spent 3 hours putting gas into the ferry tanks, having to make two trips to the refueling depot near the township of London because the agent had underestimated how much gas was in each (rusty) fuel drum. With her extra tanks nearly full for an 8-hour journey, 30TB was reared back (sitting nose-high) by the weight of the gas. That night I only got about four hours of sleep listening to a violent storm, which rolled overhead with strong winds. I was genuinely worried about weather for our flight the following day.

The weather had cleared significantly by early morning, and on my walk-around check everything appeared okay. However, shortly after take-off, it was apparent that the left main tank was only about two thirds full. Very strange. I did some calculations to see whether we had enough gas for the flight we had filed to Honolulu and reckoned that it would be okay, just be a bit tight if headwinds prevailed. The winds did prevail, and about five hours into the eight-hour flight, I amended the flight plan to Hilo, more than 100 miles short of Honolulu. I could only rationalize that with the plane in the unusual reared-back-on-her-haunches position after being refueled, some gas had spilled out of 30TB's left main tank vents during the violent winds in the night, and I missed the discrepancy on the fuel gauges before takeoff. I guess I'll never know for sure....

Another interesting aspect to this flight was that I could have filed for clearance with San Francisco Radio on the ground at Christmas Island using high frequency (HF) radio, but for the sake of expediency—I had been advised that it could take up to 45 minutes to receive clearance so you would have to wait or be delayed—I took off and requested clearance once airborne. All this from a controller who was a good 2500 nautical miles away.

On landing at Hilo, I parked at the general aviation (GA) apron and a customs official drove up and asked if I had written permission to land there. I explained that I did not have any written confirmation and had diverted to Hilo due to potential fuel shortage. This declaration is usually greeted with respect, but he said that I had landed illegally and was liable for a $5,000 fine, because I didn't have written confirmation to land in Hawaii. I had made a mistake after ringing U.S. Samoa and asking the airport guy what documentation he would require for me to land there, if I should visit from Independent Samoa. I didn't realize that a fax has to be sent to Hawaii to gain permission to land there. When I had explained what Diabetes World Flight was, the customs man asked me to wait, and he came back half an hour later with a written warning as opposed to a fine. I was very grateful indeed.

Hawaii

Hawaii is well known as American tropical bliss. And bliss it was for me. I was able to fly solo again for the first time in four and a half months. February 8th was a sunny day, perfect for a VFR (visual) departure from Honolulu International Airport. My pre-flight sugar was 115—great. Soon after takeoff, I skirted along hillsides to the north of Honolulu with its historic harbor waters glistening to the south. I was extremely happy to have the aircraft to myself again. Suddenly I had room beside me in the cockpit to organize my maps, food and blood glucose meters. It felt particularly good to aviate where it's recognized that flying can be safe with diabetes.

I had planned an exploratory flight from Honolulu northwest to the island of Kauai, then back to Oahu, skirting around the North Shore, then over to Molokai and finally to Maui to meet with Dave and Lori who had traveled all the way from Omaha to coincide our visits to Hawaii. I decided not to talk with ATC once outside Honolulu airspace. I just wanted to relax and enjoy the flight and scenery. However, I dialed in the appropriate radio frequencies, ready to use in case of emergency.

Hawaii is comprised of volcanic islands, and erosion over the millennia has resulted in some breathtaking mountain scenery. Around the north coast of Kauai, cliffs rise almost 3,000 feet sheer out of the water. Cruising at 500 feet alongside these cliffs, listening to the sightseeing helicopters' common frequency, I could see two whirlybirds in the distance coming toward me. As they closed the gap, one helicopter pilot broadcast "Can you see the fixed wing ahead?" They had spotted me. Just before whizzing overhead, the radio crackled into life once again with "Tak-a-tak-a-tak-a-tak!" We're all just boys at heart!

As they cleared behind, I descended to 30 feet over the water and wheeled around, marveling at the huge cliffs rising above. *Real* low level. This is what flying is all about—the *freedom,* the *exhilaration.*

I was enjoying myself tremendously, watching powerful Pacific swells roll by and smash into the cliff faces. They were *huge.* Having traveled more than 1,000 miles, those waves were unleashing considerable energy on the rocks. Shortly after I was fascinated to find tiny salt crystals forming on the windscreen and the black leading edges of the wings. These were from fine spray just above the water's surface. (I wiped them off at the end of the flight for fear of corrosion.)

Turning back toward Oahu at low level, I noticed an area of disturbed water ahead, a cauldron of foaming, frothy white. I wondered what on earth (or sea) this could be. Was it possibly a breaching whale? I thought about this. A humpback whale can be 70 feet in length, and when breaching, much of their body is out of the water. Here I was at 30 feet having lots of fun. A whale rising less than half its length would hit the plane! Instinctively, I eased up to 50 feet. You could explain a bird strike, but not a "whale strike."

I returned southeast across 50 miles of open water to Oahu, and tested my blood sugar—151, fine. At one point on the trip, it was hazy enough, and I was low enough that I couldn't see land anywhere. This had been the case during previous flights over the vast Pacific Ocean, but somehow at these low levels around Hawaii's islands, it almost seemed lonelier. The North Shore of Oahu soon appeared in the haze ahead, and I skirted round to the northeast, keeping far enough out to sea at one stage to clear military airspace. I wheeled around a few times, drinking in views of Oahu's craggy volcanic landscape.

I crossed over to the south side of Molokai, and in the lee of northerly trade winds, the water was almost mirror-calm near the shores. Down at low level, I noticed another clear disturbance on the water surface ahead. I pulled up a little and looked down, awe-struck to see a humpback whale with her calf blowing a stream of white spray into the air. Now *this* really was amazing. I had never seen a whale in the wild. I circled the area, fascinated by these graceful mammals. Over the next 30 miles, I saw several more whales gliding along slowly. One large whale swam on its side, playfully slapping its pectoral fin on the water surface.

Just as with the sharks and dolphins in Shark Bay, it took considerable willpower to leave these humpbacks behind and land at Kahalui Airport on Maui. It was a truly memorable flight. Blood sugars ran from 115, 151 to 158 and finally 185, all well within the flying range of 100–300. I had flown around several of Hawaii's stunning islands, lapped up terrific volcanic scenery, reveled at low level, and witnessed one of the world's most amazing wonders—humpback whales on the water's surface. I was flying solo again. This was freedom—what flying is all about.

En-Route Blood Sugar Control

Despite the organizational stress of the first month, bouts of intense frustration, plus a few hair-raising moments during the months of flying, the U.S. system of frequent blood sugar testing ensured that my overall diabetes control was safe for flying.

I took 250 tests in total during 63 flights and 187 hours logged flying, and recorded each result. None of the tests were above the maximum 300 level for flying, while 16 results were below the lower limit of 100. Whenever low, I would ingest at least 20 g of carbs to bring my blood sugars back up. The lowest reading was 69 mg/dl, only just below a normal (non-diabetic) blood sugar reading. On no occasion was I concerned about my blood sugar control when flying. (In Australia one result came in at 60, much lower than expected given that the previous test had been well above 100. I re-tested immediately and discovered that the reading of 60 had been a rogue test result. I was still above 100.)

Twice in Australia my blood sugar was below 100 for the pre-flight test. This delayed takeoff by 20 minutes while I chewed on some candy and waited for blood sugars to rise above 100. It was extremely hot and possibly the heat had increased the uptake of insulin and lowered my blood sugar faster than anticipated. I decided to add another test an hour before estimated take-off. If I was below, or it looked like I may be lowering toward 100, I would eat some candy. This seemed to sort out the pre-flight tests and avoided any further takeoff delays.

Half-way around the flight, in Thailand, my A1C was 5.6%. This was the best A1C test result I'd ever had, and within a normal (non-diabetic) range of 4.3–5.8%. I believe this is a true testament to the benefits of the frequent blood sugar testing that I carried out during DWF.

People have asked me if I took an alarm clock to remember the hourly in-flight tests. With the exception of two short delays in testing each successive hour, I found I could remember without an independent reminder. When flying long distances on a flight plan, I needed to update navigation progress, check engine instruments, and communicate regularly with air traffic control. This constant monitoring fostered a disciplined environment, with hourly testing becoming part of the cockpit routine. On the longer flights over water, and over India, I had to radio position reports every hour. This acted as a natural reminder to test blood sugars each hour into these flights.

Blood Sugar Control During Hairy/Stressful Moments

There is no doubt that the highest blood sugar readings during Diabetes World Flight coincided with the most stressful moments. The Hawaii-California flight showed consecutive readings of 225 and 221 in the first three hours of the flight from Hilo to San Francisco. These were the hours of the most stressful flying of the project, as I battled with the controls in turbulent cloud while trying to avoid overstressing the overweight airframe carrying a full load of gas. My blood sugars took a few hours to return to normal on that 11-hour flight.

The second highest reading of all the flights was a 263 after a frustrating delay at Goose Bay where we had to depart by a certain time or have to pay a landing fee in Greenland that was triple in cost. The highest reading of the world flight was 267 mg/dl after an intensely frustrating delay on the ground in Iceland.

Altitude and Blood Sugars

At higher altitudes, the heart needs to work harder (beating faster) to pump rarified oxygen around the body. This can result in lower blood sugars and medical advice is to reduce insulin to offset this physiological reaction. Our highest flight was at 15,000 feet for almost six hours over stunning desert landscapes of Saudi Arabia. I took seven tests during this flight, the results of which were 137 (pre-takeoff test), 160, 83, 115, 74, 94 and 94. As you can see, four results were *below* the required level of 100. Even though I ingested at least 20 g of carbohydrate on each occasion, the last two readings remained below 100.

This was the highest altitude flight by far. The average cruise height of the whole flight was around 7,000 feet, with a few exhilarating flights at low level. Being at an altitude of 7,000 feet can affect blood sugars if you are carrying out energetic activities on the ground, such as skiing in mountains. However, I was always sitting in the cockpit and expending little energy except for switching the ferry tank levers. Perhaps breathing portable oxygen on the highest altitude flight allowed my heart to pump more normally.

I learned early in 2002 that conventional blood glucose meters lose accuracy at higher altitudes. Some are accurate (with 20% variance of accuracy) up to 7,000 feet, others to 10,000 feet. The good thing is that meters will usually under-read the higher you go. If a test result is 60 mg/dl and you're at 10,000 feet, your actual blood sugar may be around 72 mg/dl. This is the safer way around. You'll be further from hypo than a result indicates.

Language Challenges

The official international air traffic control language is English, and, in theory, communication should not be a problem. In practice, however, there can be difficulties understanding local accents. This happened a few times in the Middle East, frequently over India, and we had quite an incident arriving in Noumea, New Caledonia, misunderstanding French accents.

In several countries domestic pilots were speaking local languages. This made me quite uncomfortable at times, as I didn't know where the other aircraft were or what they might be doing. This dual-language difficulty was especially noticeable while flying over Italian airspace on the way to Malta from France, and in New Caledonia in the Pacific Ocean.

In the Middle East, there were a few occasions when I had to ask ATC to repeat what they had said. Fortunately there are many jargon words used in aviation, so it was possible to understand eventually. Over Saudi Arabia I often communicated with American expatriates (it almost felt like U.S. airspace at times). Occasionally in the Middle East, we heard "Inshallah" at the end of a transmission, meaning, "As Allah wills it."

Over India, the accents we heard were particularly challenging, and Ty found he couldn't understand a single word on occasions. I remembered in my younger days watching a British television comedy *It Ain't Half Hot Mum* about British Army life in India. Perhaps I had gained an "ear" for the Indian accent from this comedy, as I found I could eventually work out what was being said by Indian ATC. However, for Ty's benefit, I would often confirm with ATC that my understanding was correct. If I did something wrong, as a legally required safety pilot, it was Ty's license at stake.

The worst misunderstanding came in New Caledonia where the French accent was particularly heavy. On January 12th, I flew a 640-mile straight-line flight from Brisbane, landing first of all at Tontouta, New Caledonia's main international airport, to clear customs and immigration formalities. As we disembarked, a charming lady walked up to the plane and then hosted us through immigration and customs. In no time at all, it seemed, we were on our way to Magenta Airport, just 20 miles to the south and right beside the capital city of Noumea.

Before taking off I spent a few minutes in Tontouta's operations room, studying local visual approach procedures and chatting with the duty officer. However, on the way to Magenta at 2,000 feet, I couldn't understand what ATC was instructing us to do. In turn, they couldn't seem to understand what I was saying. I blurted a few "Say again" requests before reporting "November Three Zero Tango Bravo, overhead 2,000 feet" at which point, ATC cleared me to land. I was grateful for ATC's understanding. This had been a real "duff up" in communication, and I suspect we were close to infringing a few New Caledonia local flight procedures.

As we taxied in, Yannick, our host while in New Caledonia, waited patiently and marshaled me to a parking spot. Shortly after we shut down, a tall distinguished-looking gentleman strode up determinedly and spoke rather intensely with Yannick in French. A few sharp gestures and cold glances flew my way. *Hmmm—something was up.* Indeed it was. This gentleman was the CEO of the local aviation authority, and he'd been flying when he heard our labored ATC communication, misunderstandings and somewhat non-standard approach.

Yannick was a retired senior aviation authority official and knew the CEO well. After a few minutes, the gesticulations slowed and the atmosphere lightened. The silver-haired CEO strode away, looking a little happier. I have no doubt that Yannick smoothed over some potentially stormy waters for which I am extremely grateful.

Hassles

Some of the more stressful moments of DWF coincided with the receipt, or delayed receipt, of clearances to fly into certain countries in the Middle East, Asia and the Pacific. India was delayed by a couple of days, and we had to wait in Muscat, Oman—albeit in a comfortable Sheraton Hotel that sponsored DWF. Then Thailand strangely delayed its clearance until the day before we were to fly from Calcutta to Bangkok. (Apparently Thailand does this quite often with small aircraft, and as a result, planning can be a nightmare.) When I eventually received the faxed clearance, there was a mistake with the dates. I just went the following day and, fortunately, was able to sort the problem out after arriving.

On many occasions, just getting through an airport was quite an ordeal. It could take hours to pay landing and navigation fees, collect weather reports, file a flight plan and refuel the plane. In Bombay Airport, it took four hours of mind-boggling hassle to get through after making a six-hour flight from Oman. Including Muscat Airport departure formalities, the journey from Oman took 13 hours to complete door-to-door—an exhausting trip. It is interesting to note that I was challenged to show my pilot's license and medical certificate only once on the whole trip, and this was on arriving in Hilo, Hawaii, when sorting out admin difficulties and avoiding a $5,000 fine.

Not receiving the trip kits (charts and airport instrument approach details) on time in Iceland and Greece caused a terrible fluster and required immense patience. The package arrived in Iceland the day after we left, and then strangely went to Sweden before catching up with me in London 10 days later. That said, the Jeppessen service was terrific once everything was back on track.

Funnily enough, our arrival at every single Pacific Island resulted in an incident of one kind or another. In Fiji I was told I'd landed illegally, and momentarily, it seemed like jail was beckoning. In Samoa, it was impossible to pass through passport control and customs. The staff had gone home between shifts. In Hawaii, I did not have the correct paperwork and was threatened with a $5,000 fine.

I was amused to read copies of the Sunday *Scottish Daily Record* weekly reports of my progress across the Pacific. The newspaper had been using my website diary details plus email contact to write articles. The Pacific Island hassles were sensationalized quite nicely. However, by this stage of the project, I was resigned to any admin challenges. All I could do was try to sort them out as best as possible whenever I encountered them—and try not to get too frustrated. Fortunately there was no rush; I didn't have any pressing time constraints.

> *Flying around the world is like raising kids. When you've finally figured out how to do it the right way, you've finished.*
> —Ron Bower, who has flown around
> the world solo in a helicopter

The Longest Flight—Hawaii to San Francisco

The flight between Hawaii and San Francisco was a particularly meaningful flight. I was able to fly it solo. And at 2026 nautical miles, it was the longest single flight, estimated at around 12 hours. This would be useful in demonstrating that a pilot with diabetes can carry out a challenging endurance flight safely.

While my Class III medical clearly states *Not valid outside the borders of the USA,* I had checked with aviation lawyers and the FAA medical branch to be sure I could fly this 12-hour leg without a safety pilot. I discovered that the flight plan could be filed as either international or domestic. If domestic, there was no need for a safety pilot. It was an easy choice. I really wanted to do this long flight on my own. The messages about flying safely with diabetes would be much stronger as a result.

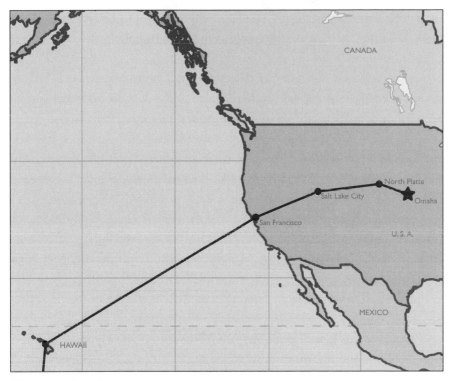

Hawaii – Omaha

There were a couple of things to do the day before setting off for California. First, the ferry tanks sat behind the center of gravity (c of g) and, therefore, when they were full, the aircraft c of g would be out of limits—too far back. To bring the c of g back within limits, 200 pounds of ballast had to be stowed in the nose luggage hold. By the time the fuel burned off, the c of g would move all the way to the forward limit. The aircraft would then fly "nose low" requiring lots of rear trim. I wrote up a detailed computer spreadsheet calculation of c of g movements from start to finish, ensuring I would not be out of limits at any stage of this long flight. After the ferry tanks were drained, I planned to push a heavy bag from the front, over the tank tops and down into the rear of the cabin. This would bring the c of g a little further back, just for extra safety.

What could I use as ballast? The best thing was lead shot. However, the best I could find at a local Hilo shopping mall was bags of compost. I put each into a separate plastic bag to protect them against moisture, and punctured each inside bag with small holes in case any air trapped inside expanded at height and burst through. Then I bought provisions, lots of decent carbohydrate snacks. My favorite was Nutri-Grain bars, with plenty of carbohydrate but high in fiber, raising blood sugars relatively slowly. I also had plenty of candy in case I needed to increase blood sugar quickly.

A 38-pound life raft was positioned behind the two seats, squashed up against the ferry tanks. I had practiced opening the door from inside, getting out of the cockpit onto the wing, and reaching inside to drag the raft out. It was tough, but possible, assuming I was not injured. A red lanyard line was attached to a bracket above the door to ensure that once it was thrown into the water, the raft would not blow away. The rope was designed to break as the plane sank.

Finally, I reviewed the flight plan and confirmed weather conditions for February 14th with the flight service station. Strong tailwinds were forecast en-route with some bad weather nearby associated with a cold front that extended hundreds of miles to the east-northeast. The forecast for Hayward in the San Francisco Bay area was for rain but the cloud base would be a comfortable 2,000 feet.

One thing I was very strict about was ensuring that the first five hours would be in daylight. This was one of the most dangerous times for DWF, as one engine failure would result in a forced ditching in the water below. On takeoff, N30TB would weigh over 6,400 pounds, 19% "overgross," (over normal maximum weight). It would take five hours of hand-flying (the autopilot could not be used when the plane was over normal weight) to burn enough gas to get down to normal maximum gross weight of 5,400 pounds. When this happened, N30TB could fly okay on one engine. I decided to fly the next morning, weather permitting, taking off before 1 p.m. to ensure five daylight hours.

A few final tasks remained: Arrange for an agricultural inspector to inspect the plane and receive a written confirmation that I was not carrying any banned food (such as fruit) from Hawaii. And fill up the gas tanks. These would have to be done just before departing.

I woke up at 4 a.m. to check weather conditions over the telephone in case I could leave at dawn. The weather forecast still showed a low-pressure system to the north with an associated cold front extending several hundred miles to the east-northeast. There would be headwinds for the first few hours, and from a third of the way, tailwinds would pick up to 45 knots. Near the frontal zone at two sections there would be cloud with possible embedded thunderstorms. With net tailwinds, I could deviate to the south of the direct route and keep clear of the frontal zone. I took a deep breath and decided to depart late morning, and then filed my domestic flight plan over the telephone.

At 10 a.m. I was standing by the airplane. The fuel truck came over and the main tanks were filled. I unscrewed the filler cap on each ferry tank inside the cabin, stretched a plastic extension tube over the gas hose and filled up the two ferry tanks. It was a cumbersome job, squatting on the pilot seats and stretching into the back to insert the tube into the tank, taking great care not to spill gas inside the plane. Before doing this, I positioned a plastic bucket under the tail. As the ferry tanks filled up, the c of g moved a long way back, and I had been warned that the Baron could tip up and dent its tail on the ground. She didn't tip back, but she wasn't far off. The nose sat a good foot higher than normal with the nose strut abnormally extended. The Baron looked like a rearing horse!

The agriculture officer came out and had a quick look in the cabin while I signed off the forms. Just before 11 a.m., I walked around the aircraft and carried out my pre-flight check. The six fuel drains were clear of contamination, engine oil levels were healthy and the compost bags for ballast secure in the nose luggage bay. I took the pitot tube cover off and checked that the intake hole was clear. (If there was an obstruction in it, the airspeed indicator would not work.) I checked the hinges and brackets of the ailerons, rudder and elevator control surfaces, and that the wing-tank gas caps were secure. The tires had been pumped up an extra 5 psi in Brisbane for the heavy weight of the extra gas. I checked that these were okay. Finally I shone a torch into the wheel bay to check that the undercarriage had not chafed the temporary ferry tank piping as they retracted or extended.

Everything appeared to be in order. There were three blood glucose meters in the cockpit and plenty of test strips. I double-checked food and drink provisions—more than enough. I tested my blood sugar. It was 100. I ate a sandwich, 30 g of carbohydrate. I was ready to go.

As the second engine fired up, the airflow hit the elevators, and the Baron's nose tilted forwards. *That's better!* I requested clearance for my IFR flight to Hayward Executive Airport. I first had to wait 10 minutes for a Naval Orion surveillance plane taxiing for departure. Then the clearance came through "Cleared to Hayward as filed" and I taxied for the long north-westerly runway. The longer the runway the better—it was needed to get this heavy airplane off the ground. I then carried out the pre-takeoff checks and engine run-ups near the runway threshold.

Just before midday, I lined up on the runway and opened the throttles. Being 19% over normal maximum weight, the Baron accelerated slowly down the runway. I passed through the normal rotate speed of 80 knots and waited for 100 knots before pulling back on the controls, gently raising the nose and rising off the ground. (The extra weight would increase the stall speed. It was safer to rotate with more speed in hand.) As the 104 knots "best climb" speed was maintained, the Baron settled into an initial climb rate of 800 feet per minute—not bad for a heavy bird!

I climbed up to 7,000 feet and settled in for a long cruise. It was necessary to keep a close eye on the ground speed displayed on the GPS and also the time to destination. If headwinds were greater than expected and tailwinds delayed, the amount of fuel remaining could be tight. If this happened, I would decide before the halfway point whether to continue on or to turn back. It was clear air at first, with layers of gray cloud gradually building up above me. About 15 minutes into the flight, the Naval Orion passed down my starboard side in the opposite direction, wheeled to the right, passed behind and departed to the north. It was like a slow farewell salute.

Soon I was drifting in and out of layered cloud, and less than an hour into the flight, I was totally enveloped. There was no outside horizon to fly toward, so I had to focus on the instruments to keep straight and level flight. I was hand-flying the plane, checking the GPS often, and making sure I was on direct track for the next required reporting points. Two hours into the flight, it was raining and bumpy. Almost immediately, ATC gave a chill warning. There was a squall line near my route. These are lines of intense thunderstorms, and apart from tornadoes, represent the single greatest risk to aircraft if you are caught inside one. I plotted the coordinates. The squall line sat parallel to the cold front but well to the south, disturbingly close to my track. Immediately I turned 10 degrees to the right to try to keep clear of these dangerous thunderstorms.

The next hour was harrowing. By now the weather radar was showing heavy rain returns all around, so there was no way to detect and steer around embedded thunderstorms. I just had to wait and see what happened. Although I had burned off two hours of gas, I was still more than 600 pounds overweight and worried about overstressing the airframe. Normally the maximum indicated speed in the Baron is 225 knots, but since she was overweight with the extra gas, I set a temporary limit at 150 knots maximum speed. The airframe could be overstressed easily, so I needed to avoid high speed and turbulence. At around 60% power, I was cruising at 145 knots indicated airspeed, so I could easily exceed 150 knots in turbulent air.

The turbulence was severe at times, and I had to throttle back several times to avoid going too fast in turbulent updrafts. At times it was a battle to keep the aircraft wings level. One updraft was so powerful, I was buffeted 500 feet higher while the throttles were closed, literally gliding. The airplane shuddered and shook. My head rocked violently at times, but at least in tandem with the cockpit. I could still (just) read the artificial horizon and try to keep the wings level. A minute later my speed dropped off violently, and even with almost full power, I was pushed 900 feet down. All I could do now was try to maintain upright flight and keep the aircraft from going too slow and stalling in powerful downdrafts. Any height deviations had to be accepted. I quietly thought about this disturbing situation. If the turbulence got worse, I could be sitting cozily in the cockpit one instant, and the next be outside flapping my arms. It was one of the most frightening moments of my flying career.

Half an hour later, the turbulence began to taper off, the clouds thinned, and eventually I was in clear and calm air. It was good to relax. I flew another two hours manually, and then engaged the autopilot. Once the autopilot was on, I took my hands off the controls, sat back and contemplated this flight. I was now a good 750 miles offshore. The water below would be getting colder as I headed northeastward. At least if one engine failed now, I could stay aloft and make my way back to Hilo. Despite this, I felt remote and lonely. And I was getting further away from land.

Certain emergency profiles can prey on one's mind. One is an engine fire in a twin-engine piston aircraft. If it is not extinguished immediately, it can take just two minutes to burn through the wing spar and lead to disaster. One strong recommendation is to land as soon as you possibly can if a fire starts. At this moment in time, it would mean ditching in increasingly remote sea areas. These issues are what professional ferry pilots constantly deal with. I have the utmost respect for them.

I constantly checked the engine instruments: engine oil pressure, oil temperature, cylinder head temperature, exhaust gas temperatures, fuel remaining is okay, and "electrics" are okay. No warning lights are illuminated, such as the alternator or vacuum pump for the pressure instruments (artificial horizon, directional gyro). I occasionally looked out to the engine nacelles. If any oil was leaking out, I could possibly see it. I checked that the airplane was on track according to the GPS flight plan. If not, then turn toward and re-establish the direct track. Every hour I had to give an "Operations Normal" report to San Francisco Radio, with position and time.

Despite flying on instruments in cloud for the first three hours and battling with the controls in turbulence, I managed to test my blood sugar three times. It took some manual dexterity, mind you, but it was possible. The results were higher than normal at 189, 225 and 221—most likely stress contributed toward these high readings.

After four hours, the weather cleared and a vivid crimson sun set behind the plane. Tailwinds began to build, and my groundspeed increased by the minute. *Great!* My flight time would be less than 12 hours and well within my 15 hours endurance.

After five hours, darkness fell. I passed through a few banks of cloud illuminated by moonlight. Then it cleared to reveal bright stars above. The moon seemed to be smiling benevolently, as if confirming perfect flying conditions. The red anti-collision light on top of the tail fin whirred around incessantly, casting a red hue over the wings and engine nacelles every few seconds. I felt secure in the cockpit, engines humming consistently, instrument dials glowing reassuringly.

I had left the cockpit heating off, not wanting to be too warm in case I became tired. Two hours off the mainland U.S., however, I was getting cold. A blanket wrapped around my legs plus a jacket was not enough. I flew into a thin layer of cloud, and the outside temperature reduced to freezing level. I switched on the bright ice-lights that illuminated the wings to find a light layer of ice on the wing leading edges and HF aerial. Time to go lower, and after gaining permission from San Francisco Radio, I descended into warmer air where the ice gradually melted. I switched on the cockpit heater. It was good to warm up.

During the 11-hour flight, I didn't feel tired. I was constantly updating the GPS navigation progress and estimated arrival time. I also kept a very close eye on the engine gauges in case anything started to go wrong. Every hour required position reports, plus a blood sugar test. There really wasn't any time to get tired.

After the first two high blood sugars of 189 and 225, I topped up with short-acting insulin. It had been turbulent, and this also took some manual dexterity between the controls, drawing up insulin and injecting. However, it worked okay. The next result was 221, followed by 194 and 207. I wasn't happy with this, so I topped up again. It was good to see sugars reducing to 164. However, the next one was up to 211. *Damn!* I topped up again. I was frustrated. Regular insulin took around 30–45 minutes to start working, and I didn't have the option of exercising shortly after injecting to lower my blood sugars more rapidly. (The insulin I use now works considerably faster and more predictably.) However, the subsequent results were 180 and then 158. My blood sugars settled down nicely for the final four results, reading 137, 122, 139 and finally 121 before landing.

During the flight I ate moderate amounts of sandwich or Nutri-Grain bar. For the first time on DWF, I drank water freely to keep hydrated. So far I had not needed to use a Little John urine pot, even on flights lasting over 8 hours. (At altitude, with less humidity, it is easy to become dehydrated. Certainly the body doesn't want to pass as much water.) Using a Little John wouldn't have been a very attractive sight, I am sure, but on my own during this long flight, it was a welcome relief—twice!

For four hours I could not contact San Francisco Radio but managed to relay position reports via VHF emergency guard frequency with three airliners flying overhead—Flights Hawaii 20, Fedex 1800 and American 72. It was lonely flying out of contact for so long over such remote and cold seas. During one radio relay, the pilot asked me what I was up to in a Baron, so I explained. It was good to talk.

Close to California, tailwinds were cracking along at 45 knots, pushing ground speed up to a steady 220 knots. The forecast for Hayward Airport was extremely accurate, with cloud base at 2,500 feet and good visibility. NORCAL (Northern California) Approach prompted me for my desired instrument approach. I selected the VOR approach. Hayward was not manned overnight, so descending through cloud on the steep VOR approach, I pressed the "transmit" button seven times on the airfield frequency to switch the runway lights on. At exactly at 2,500 feet, I broke out of cloud. I was high, but instead of making a gut-wrenching dive for the runway, I made a leisurely overhead approach, descending gently downwind to land on runway 28.

I was tired after this 11-hour flight from Hawaii but immensely happy and relieved to have finished the over-water Pacific flights. Three more flights remained to get me home to Omaha. It was time to anticipate finishing DWF, safely and in one piece.

> *The difference between perseverance and obstinacy is that one comes from a strong will and one comes from a strong won't.*
> —Henry Ward Beecher

Time Zones

A few people asked me how I coped with managing diabetes across so many time zones during the flight. However, time zones were never really an issue as the maximum time difference on any one flight was only two hours—between Hawaii and San Francisco. All the rest were only one-hour time zones. It did feel, however, odd and potentially confusing to cross the international dateline three times in the Pacific Ocean. The first time we gained a day, arriving in Samoa 20 hours before taking off from Fiji. Conversely we lost a day on arriving in Christmas Island, arriving 32 hours after taking off eight hours earlier. It took some detailed calculations to keep track of the time and dates.

Reactions to DWF

Throughout DWF people were extremely supportive and encouraging. There was only one person who was negative, interestingly enough, an aviation authority doctor. When I told him what I was up to, there was an audible gasp at the other end of the telephone line, followed by "I suppose you're going to try to get lots of publicity and embarrass us." I didn't say anything. His comment seemed to suggest that he *should* be embarrassed. I think he realized how defensive he had sounded, and as if by magic, he was suddenly very encouraging.

Loulla Constantinidou in Cyprus asked me, "Are you scared of failing?" It was a great question. If I suffered an unexpected severe hypo and ended up in hospital, it could have jeopardized the whole project. Loulla wondered if I was worried about failing given that members of the diabetes community were following my progress. I thought carefully about this. Overall I felt comfortable with my diabetes control, because I test my sugars frequently and that helped me avoid severe lows. I had found the U.S. system for flying with diabetes to be safe and practical. There was definitely a risk that I could fall ill while traveling and encounter difficulties with diabetes control. This would have to be dealt with if and when it happened. If anything, managing diabetes was the one controllable risk attached to DWF. I felt that the risk of mechanical failure of the aircraft was less controllable. You can maintain a plane's engine but not continually test its integrity as you can with your blood sugar. And if I crashed in a remote spot because of mechanical failure, it would be easy for people to assume that the accident was diabetes related. I therefore tried hard to ensure thorough maintenance was carried out all the way around the world.

Two people felt sorry for me. One was the airport manager at Fiji's Faleolo Airport. He read a newspaper article outlining the loss of my flying career, and felt it was sad that I had to resort to a world flight to prove a point about flying safely with diabetes. And he felt sorry for me that I could not pursue a normal flying career. The other person was 17-year old Steph Speer who'd had diabetes since the age of two. She said she felt sorry for me being diagnosed at 25 and losing an established flying career. She felt it would have been better to grow up with diabetes and be used to it when entering adulthood. It was a fascinating comment. There are added challenges to growing up with diabetes, such as growth hormone masking the uptake of insulin and making diabetes control more difficult during puberty. Parents of young children worry about the dangers of severe hypoglycemia, ketoacidosis, and debilitating long-term complications. They can feel a whole range of emotions, from guilt and intense sorrow to frustration and anger. It can be difficult to pass on the responsibility of managing diabetes to the child. I avoided the added challenges of diabetes in childhood, and my parents did not have to be directly involved. Indeed, I can still be wistful about losing an aviation career, but I'm extremely grateful to have had the opportunity to fly fast-jets in the RAF. If I had been diagnosed as a child, I never would have had the chance.

Day 159—The Final Flight

It felt a little strange to be into the final days. It had taken 159 days to reach Nebraska and almost a year since beginning preparations. However, the final day was crisp and clear, a perfect day for completing Diabetes World Flight. I was extremely happy to be finishing, safely and in one piece.

The final flight was a quick one-hour hop from North Platte, Nebraska, to Omaha. It was only 30°F as I carried out the walk-around check for the last flight. It was such a change from Australia's searing outback and its zillion flies or the tropical storms on Christmas Island.

A local television station reporter came out to the airport and filmed me strapping in, firing up the engines and taxiing out. After takeoff, I turned east and into bright morning sunshine. Nebraska's dry winter countryside looked barren, but before long, dust-colored fields transformed into a homogenous mass of snow-covered land. Flying over Omaha, I peered into the distance but couldn't pick out Council Bluffs' runway. My GPS map told me where the airfield was, but I just couldn't see it. Snow made the view entirely different from the summer landscape I had left.

Suddenly I saw it ahead. I switched from Omaha Approach to Council Bluffs' frequency and positioned downwind runway 13. I dived down, accelerating to 180 knots ground speed as I leveled off 30 feet above the runway. It was great to finish the way I had started—with some adrenaline flowing! As I pulled up and lowered the landing gear and flaps for landing, I felt powerful emotions. When I had taken off five months earlier, I had no idea how the flight would work out—whether I would even survive. Now I was arriving where I had begun. Diabetes World Flight was finishing successfully. It felt like I had truly "come home."

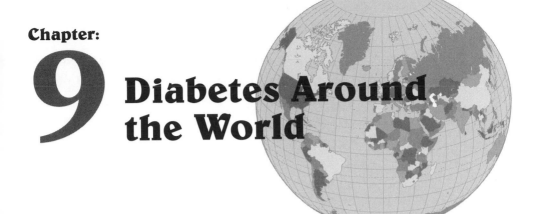

9 Diabetes Around the World

There is an epidemic going on.
> —Dr. Mohamed El-Zaheri, President,
> The Jordanian Society for the Care of Diabetes

I don't know what your destiny will be, but one thing I do know: the only ones among you who will be really happy are those who have sought and found how to serve.
> —Albert Schweitzer

During my five-month journey I passed through 22 countries and met with diabetes associations in 19 of these. It was probably the most informative five months I have ever spent. I came away with my eyes opened to:
- the effects of lifestyle on the growing epidemic of type 2 diabetes
- what happens to people with diabetes when a healthcare system gets overburdened
- the discrimination and stigma attached to diabetes in many countries
- what happens when people cannot pay for their diabetes supplies
- how difficult life can be with diabetes in different parts of the world

I learned much about type 2 diabetes. First, it is truly a worldwide epidemic, with numbers increasing at alarming rates. Genes play a powerful role in diabetes, as I saw in many countries, but there must also be an environmental trigger to make it manifest. One of the most common triggers is lifestyle choices that lead to weight gain and little or no exercise. Again, without exception, in every country where people have begun to move into the cities and have adopted a more Western diet of refined foods and a sedentary lifestyle, the numbers of overweight and obese people are going up. When people are thick about the middle, insulin can't do its job, and blood sugar levels go up. This is called insulin resistance, and is the first step on the road to type 2 diabetes. This is also a *giant* step toward heart disease and cancer, according to the World Health Organization. Even if you don't have the genes for diabetes, your heart risk skyrockets with obesity, as does your risk of developing cancer, such as breast and colon cancer.

> *The best measure of a man's honesty isn't his income tax return.*
> *It's the zero adjust on his bathroom scale.*
>
> —Arthur C. Clarke

Even in Great Britain and the United States, richer diets, often with increased junk food, and more sedentary jobs and lifestyle are regarded as the prime cause of increased incidence of type 2 diabetes, heart disease, and cancer. Just a few generations ago, a much larger percentage of the population in every country lived and worked on the land. Now we work in offices, sitting on our backsides in front of computers, drinking coffee and eating snacks. People watch more and more television. It's not just a middle-age syndrome. Now we have obese kids being diagnosed with type 2 diabetes. And they are beginning to experience serious complications such as heart attacks in their 20s. Diabetes and heart disease go hand in hand, even for people who are not overweight. This is not a healthy direction for any society to take. Another thing I learned is that one of the ironies about improved healthcare extending the lifespan of people around the world is that people are now living long enough for their pancreas to wear out...long enough to develop type 2 diabetes.

Some countries have a distinct shortage of doctors and healthcare facilities but must take care of enormous populations. In other countries, people cannot afford their insulin supplies. The efforts of the International Diabetes Federation (IDF), country diabetes associations and many other organizations are to be applauded. They are working hard to make people aware and to improve the lives of people with diabetes. We may not have found a cure for diabetes, but we do have the tools and the knowledge to manage diabetes wherever it appears. We need to get this knowledge and these tools to everyone who needs them.

Rising Numbers and Awareness

At every diabetes association or diabetes clinic, I was told how type 2 diabetes numbers are shooting through the roof. Even in Iceland where the incidence of diabetes is just 2% of the population, numbers are increasing at alarming rates. Numbers are increasing around the world so quickly that the IDF has estimated that more than 333 million people will have diabetes by 2025 compared to 194 million today.

There are shocking diabetes statistics in the Middle East. On the second day in Jordan, I managed to locate the Jordanian Society for the Care of Diabetes office in a quiet back street in Amman and met with the Society President, Dr. Mohamed El-Zaheri. Two recent independent studies of diabetes and impaired glucose tolerance (IGT) in Jordan's over 25 year olds concluded that 14% had diabetes and 11% had IGT. Published figures for Lebanon, Kuwait, Saudi Arabia, Syria, Egypt and Oman showed identical figures. Dr. El Zaheri outlined that the past 30 years have shown a near epidemic in Jordan, primarily due to changes in lifestyle—changing diet (higher refined carbohydrates and fat content) and being more sedentary, leading to higher incidence of overweight, and in turn, to type 2 diabetes.

In the Sheraton Hotel in Bahrain, I took part in a press conference with Dr. Salwa Al Mahroos, the Vice President of the Bahrain Diabetic Society. One research project concluded that 20% of the Bahrain population over 50 years of age had diabetes, a frightening number. Additionally, type 1 diabetes, usually seen in children, was accelerating, while alarmingly, type 2 diabetes, normally seen in middle age, was increasingly diagnosed among juveniles.

There are significant side-effects for any country with high numbers of people with diabetes—even for industrialized nations like the U.S. and the U.K., but smaller nations are feeling a huge strain daily. Malta's medical resources are stretched at the seams. The Maltese Diabetes Association can offer free blood tests and reduced price test strips but only once a week at their office in the historic capital city of Valletta. (They kindly invited me to their annual fundraising ball in Valletta while I was there.) Both diabetes associations in Malta and Cyprus play an important role in diagnosing new cases of type 2 diabetes. In Cyprus, Loulla Constantinidou had arranged "awareness days" at her company where several colleagues had been diagnosed.

The problem is that many people have diabetes for years without knowing it. The tragedy is that long-term complications can develop during that time. Studies suggest that people have type 2 diabetes for an average of *seven* years before being diagnosed. Symptoms can be muted (as opposed to acute symptoms normally seen with type 1), and people may not register a gradual onset of general fatigue and more frequent urination. The messages are clear. Everyone who knows must spread awareness of diabetes and its symptoms, so that people can recognize them sooner and take action to return to normal blood sugar levels. Whether you have diabetes or not, a gift you can give yourself and others is a healthier diet and daily exercise.

Parents and Children with Diabetes

In many countries, the leading volunteers and most enthusiastic fundraisers are parents of children with diabetes. In Malta and Cyprus, the diabetes association committee members are mainly doctors and parents of kids with diabetes. In Cyprus, Loulla Constantinidou was driven to raise awareness after her son, George, was diagnosed with type 1 at the age of 11. Loulla offered me two interesting observations. One was that her son "lost his childhood" the day he was diagnosed. "He suddenly had to grow up," she said, getting used to daily injections, testing blood sugars and adopting a healthy diet. She also classified parents of children with diabetes as having "type 3 diabetes." It's true; it affects the whole family. Diet often has to change for everyone at home, and day-to-day care involves at least one parent full time.

Discrimination

In many countries insulin-dependent diabetes can prevent you from pursuing certain careers, including flying, police work and military service. For people with well-controlled diabetes, it can be a bitterly frustrating issue. But in some countries it is worse, with discrimination preventing people even from holding normal office jobs. People have asked me if diabetes ever affected my new career. I am happy to say, no, it did not. Diabetes UK in Britain explains that although most of us with diabetes do not consider ourselves disabled, we are protected by the 1995 Disability Discrimination Act (DDA). In business and industry, people are viewed on an individual basis as to whether they can carry out a job. However, a number of occupations are not covered by the DDA, including the military, fire services, offshore jobs (at sea or on oil platforms), jobs involving heights and even competing as a horse jockey—and of course, flying careers. Even though I was working before DDA was enacted, I didn't come across any discrimination.

In Cyprus I met with George, a young man in his mid 20s with type 1 diabetes. Soon after graduating from University, George went on a job interview and presented a résumé (CV) showing that he was a member of the Cyprus Diabetes Association. When asked why, his answer was simple. He had type 1 diabetes, and his mother, Loulla, was an active member as well. Shortly afterward, George was dropped from the application shortlist, without any explanation. He knew it would be difficult to prove but felt sure that discrimination was the case. He was understandably frustrated. His diabetes was well controlled, and he was perfectly capable of carrying out the job he had applied for. Indeed, he had gained a top degree at a British university and was extremely well qualified for the position. Fortunately, George found a first-class (similar) job at a different company.

One of the most moving anecdotes about employment discrimination was in a message I received on my website guest page, summing up a young lady's experience in India: *I am mighty thrilled to read about Douglas and have already emailed him to say so. It is indeed an achievement that U.K. has modified its laws to permit juvenile diabetics to fly aircraft. Sadly, here in India, due to lack of awareness, juvenile diabetes is looked upon as a stumbling block and one is often dissuaded from taking up routine desk jobs. To think of taking the task of piloting a plane is too far-fetched. I myself have been refused by a few banks for desk jobs though the concerned organizations took great care not to admit this fact in as many words. But, the moment you mention you are a diabetic, they drop you like a hot brick. Ignorance, insensitivity or plain callousness—call it what you wish to....*

Discrimination can be bitterly frustrating. We have to work hard to improve people's knowledge and help stamp out unnecessary and unacceptable workplace discrimination.

Access to healthcare in some countries is even worse. After finishing DWF, I attended the IDF Annual Congress in Paris where I met a doctor from Cambodia. He explained that there were no cases of juvenile diabetes outside of the cities, because children wasted away and died before any diagnosis could be made. There were hardly any healthcare facilities in the countryside, and people couldn't afford to travel to towns or cities and pay for treatment. It was a tragic situation, and how can we begin to remedy it?

The Global Diabetes Community

After completing DWF, I was, indeed, fortunate to meet so many people involved in the diabetes community and to attend several diabetes conferences including the Children With Diabetes annual meeting in the U.S. and the IDF Congress in Paris. There are people who work incredibly hard to improve the lot of people with diabetes around the world. Diabetologists, endocrinologists, diabetes educators, eye specialists, diabetes association officers and members, dietitians, researchers, healthcare workers, people with diabetes, parents of children and adults with diabetes, other family members—they all contribute. There is a vibrant global diabetes community with much to offer and much good to do.

Children with Diabetes

I was very impressed with the activities of Children With Diabetes (CWD) and their website www.childrenwithdiabetes.com. This virtual community was established by Jeff Hitchcock, an extremely likeable and dynamic character whose daughter was diagnosed with type 1 diabetes at a very young age. He wanted to create a way for children and parents to find and share information about the condition. The result is an electric atmosphere, with people working together to find improved ways to control diabetes and to allow kids to lead normal lives.

There are added challenges to managing diabetes with children. During growth spurts and adolescence, growth hormone can block the efficiency of insulin, at times resulting in wide swings in control. When I was diagnosed at age 25, my body probably didn't have many growth hormones kicking in any more. My control seemed to settle down okay, and I was able to "bash on." However, when a young child is diagnosed with diabetes, it involves the *whole family*. Parents have to manage diabetes, giving injections, testing sugars, sometimes in the middle of the night to ensure hypos are avoided. All family members may have to alter their diet and schedules. Then, when the child is older, when is the right time to hand over control? And what can you do if other kids or people discriminate against your child because of diabetes?

Parents are concerned about the careers or activities that may be forbidden to their children. This was summed up in a message from Chris A. Nelson who said: *God's blessings to you on this endeavor. My son who wants to be a pilot also has type 1 diabetes. My hope is that this flight will change the perception of diabetics and flight for years to come!*

Indeed, I truly hope that DWF can change perceptions. At present the U.S. is regarded as exceptional in its flexibility toward pilots with diabetes. This flexibility will hopefully become the norm before long. As insulin therapy continues to improve, restrictive policies may soon be a thing of the past. Even though you have diabetes, you can still put your mind to anything and *do it!*

Empowerment

Empowerment is a word I first heard at the IDF Congress in Paris in August 2003. People with a chronic disease become empowered by gaining the knowledge and skills to self-manage that disease, whether it is diabetes (or any medical condition) successfully. This word heralds a new age in medicine in which individuals, not healthcare providers, are responsible for taking care of their own disease.

At the IDF meeting, I heard a story about a patient in India who asked her doctor what her A1C was. His answer was "You don't need to know." But of course, we *do* need to know. We need to know whether it has increased or decreased since the last test, so we can identify why this is, and if diabetes control has deteriorated, then we can do something about it. At the end of the day, we are responsible for managing our own condition. The more we know, or are empowered, the better chance we have of good control and better health overall.

Working Against Discrimination

Here is a message from Barry, on my website. *I was diagnosed with type 1 on May 17, 2002. I'm 27 years old and have been in the U.S. Navy for eight and a half years. Because of diabetes, I will shortly be discharged from the military.*

I feel passionately that regulatory authorities with "blanket bans" should adopt Diabetes UK's proposal of "individual assessment based on equal opportunity." If a person's diabetes is well controlled and he or she can avoid hypos, there is no need to restrict that person from doing the job. Particularly if there is a tried-and-tested system such as that used for flying in the U.S. This applies to every career regulatory body that discriminates against people with diabetes, not just for flying.

Diabetes prevented me from continuing my boyhood dream to fly jets. But I know I can fly safely in demanding environments—just look at Diabetes World Flight. I am certain I could fly safely in commercial and even some military aviation environments. There are plenty of others who can also do this. Canada already allows pilots with well-controlled diabetes to fly in commercial two-crew operations. We need to work positively with other aviation authorities to relax prevailing restrictive policies. That's just flying. We can work positively with any career regulatory authority, using flying as an excellent example of what *can* be done, safely and in a practical manner.

Diabetes associations and bodies such as IDF around the world are working extremely hard with advocacy campaigns to alleviate unfair restrictions against people with diabetes. They advocate for people with diabetes by showing what we *can* do, and help bring about fair policies for us. Indeed, the American Diabetes Association was instrumental in persuading the FAA to allow people with diabetes to fly.

Many people have carried out inspirational feats to demonstrate what you can do with diabetes—but we need to hear more about them. My Chief Flying Instructor, Mike Cross, and his son, Will, both with type 1 diabetes, trekked to the South Pole in 2003. Michael Hunter, who has type 1 diabetes, flies aerobatic routines around the U.S. to help inspire people with diabetes. Ron Dennis sailed single-handed around the world with type 2 diabetes. Zippora Karz kept up a grueling schedule and successful ballet dancing career in New York. Nicole Johnson pursued a beauty pageant career with type 1 diabetes and became Miss America 1999, while Gary Hall went on to win Olympic gold medals swimming in Sydney and Athens after he was diagnosed with type 1. Sir Steve Redgrave in the U.K. won an Olympic gold medal in rowing in the 2000 Olympics after being diagnosed with type 1 diabetes and was ultimately awarded a knighthood for his sporting achievements. Diabetes has not stopped any of them from doing what they wanted to do.

Diabetes Research Developments

While carrying out DWF, I learned about some exciting developments regarding *prevention* for people not yet diagnosed, a *cure* for those of us living with type 1 diabetes, and exciting new tools being developed to help *improve* diabetes management and control.

I didn't know about studies aimed at trying to prevent the onset of type 1 diabetes until meeting Sonia Cooper, President of Children with Diabetes Foundation in the U.S. Individuals, like her children, can now be tested to see if they have the genes, called human leukocyte antigen (HLA), that tell if you have an increased genetic risk for developing diabetes. Researchers can also determine if a person has autoantibodies, which are markers that show the process of attacking and killing off insulin-producing beta-cells (islet cells) and causing type 1 diabetes has started. Autoantibodies can be detected many months or even years prior to the development of diabetes, and there are studies to find out if you can reverse the autoantibody/attack process from progressing. There are also studies of people who are newly diagnosed to see if it is possible to save the remaining beta cells and, perhaps, let the cells regenerate.

In Sonia's case, her middle son was diagnosed when he was one year old. Her older son developed autoantibodies when he was 11 years old. Based on research she read in grant reviews, she knew it would be safe to give her son a "cocktail" of anti-inflammatory fatty acids (DHA or omega-3 fatty acids) and some antioxidant vitamins. His autoantibodies reversed, and they are still absent five years later. Her daughter has the same high-risk genes as her son with diabetes, and she was told that the daughter had a 50/50 chance of developing autoantibodies by the age of five. As a "preventative measure," Sonia gave her young daughter a similar cocktail of anti-inflammatory fatty acids and antioxidant vitamins. Happily, as of age 10, her daughter has not developed any autoantibodies.

There are also encouraging research developments about our ability to prevent type 2 diabetes. Type 2 is often referred to as part of a lifestyle condition accompanying weight gain. Indeed this does happen in many cases, but slim people develop type 2 diabetes, too. Research has shown that inflammation precedes the development of type 2 diabetes (as measured by C-reactive proteins). Following an "anti-inflammatory" diet of omega-3 rich foods and eliminating some of the pro-inflammatory omega-6 fatty acids (as found in highly processed foods) could be a big help in restoring normal balance to the fatty acid ratios, and thereby, reduce the number of people getting type 2 diabetes. (India's diabetes association was actively promoting this theme.)

Ultimately, a cure will likely be defined as prevention of the disease. This was the case with polio. In 1954, 55,000 people in the U.S. had polio; that year, a vaccine was given nationwide. By 1957, fewer than 200 people developed polio; and in 1991, the last case of polio was reported in the U.S. It's interesting to consider that the Nobel Prize for this work was given for preventing future generations from developing polio, not for curing people who were already diagnosed.

In regard to a cure for those of us with type 1 diabetes and insulin-dependent type 2 diabetes, there are two possible paths. One would be a biomechanical cure. Insulin pumps will soon be able to communicate with continuous glucose monitors, and deliver insulin to normalize blood sugar levels automatically. Several companies are currently making progress with these closed loop systems, and when they are on the market, perhaps in as little as two years, people with diabetes will be able to lead a normal life with the help of a small pager-like machine. When blood sugar control becomes automatic, regulatory authorities will no longer have a reason to discriminate against people with diabetes.

The other path for people with diabetes is a bio-artificial solution. At present, whole pancreas transplants or transplants of just the islet cells are provided to patients suffering serious problems with control, including severe attacks of unpredictable hypoglycemia (called hypoglycemic unawareness).

In 2003, I enjoyed a fascinating visit with Bernhard Hering, a highly respected immunologist working at the University of Minnesota. In addition to working with human islets to cure people with diabetes, Bernhard is searching for a more plentiful source of islets, researching the success of porcine (pig) islet-cell transplants into monkeys. Prior to the development of human insulin analogs, people with diabetes used insulin derived from pigs on a regular basis. Having a plentiful, inexpensive source of beta cells, such as these porcine islet cells, may have far-reaching implications for islet-cell transplants for humans. (This could also help circumvent the highly political debate regarding the use of human embryonic stem cells.) However, there is still the problem of retraining the immune system. Currently, a person with a transplant must take drugs that suppress the immune system for the rest of his or her life, and these drugs have some unpleasant side-effects. There is progress in this area. One research goal is to create medications that could be given at the time of the islet-cell transplant, and then drugs would not be required for the rest of one's life.

At this time, severe hypoglycemia is the most dangerous aspect of having diabetes, and every year, far too many people die from seizures caused by hypoglycemia. Continuous glucose monitors, when they come on the market for everyone, can warn people with hypoglycemic unawareness that they are low so they can take action to get their blood sugar levels back up. This will be a significant improvement in diabetes management and control.

Chapter:
10 Reflections on DWF

Travelers are always discoverers, especially those who travel by air. There are no signposts in the air to show a man has passed that way before. There are no channels marked. The flier breaks each second into new uncharted seas.
—Anne Morrow Lindbergh, *North to the Orient,* 1935

The People

When I moved from Thailand to the U.S. in April 2002 to begin preparations, I left behind many friends and a busy, active social life. I was suddenly on my own, feeling lonely in the first few weeks when I was staying in motels with no friends around. But I was incredibly focused on the job at hand. And before long, I felt encouraged by support from old friends and new. Messages of support appeared often on the website guest page. It soon became clear that people in the U.S. have a positive attitude toward this type of endeavor.

I met Dave, Lori and Josie in Omaha who became great friends. I first spoke with Dave on Omaha Approach frequency one night in August after he detected my Scottish accent and asked me where I was from. Dave and Lori were just about to be married, just 12 miles from my parents' home in Scotland, an incredible coincidence. When they traveled to Scotland, they met my parents and got on famously. I can understand why Dave and Lori liked the Scottish Highlands. People from the Midwest have similar characteristics to West Scottish Highlanders—friendly, welcoming and down-to-earth.

At times DWF felt like a trip down memory lane, catching up with my mother and father, my sister Ann, brother-in-law Charlie and their children Fiona, Christopher and Catriona in Scotland, and friends in London, Jordan, Dubai, Bangkok, Singapore, Perth, Melbourne, Sydney, Brisbane, and Hawaii.

I was in constant contact with people by email, often organizing plans for the next part of the journey. The IDF helped out by providing several diabetes association contacts in more remote spots such as the Pacific Islands. At each destination, I was busy meeting diabetes association members and gaining media coverage. At last count, Diabetes World Flight was featured in more than 80 different media outlets around the world, including newspapers, magazines, television and radio stations. After Reuters wrote an article and posted it on their newswire, I discovered people had read articles in newspapers all the way from Edinburgh in Scotland to Hong Kong in Asia. The overall support and opportunities to meet so many people on the world flight made the whole experience very positive.

While the flight was a project of a lifetime, it was an extremely busy time while I was on the ground. I was very stressed out for the first month until finally catching up with all the admin requirements in France. At times, I suffered from a lack of sleep. The night before the flight from London to France, I was bashing away on a computer and arranging "crew cards" at 2:30 a.m. before a fitful five-hour sleep. In France, I tried to make contact with the diabetes association but that ended up being a 10-minute conversation of sorts in the pouring rain—me trying to explain my "mission" in halting school French on an intercom with a woman in an apartment upstairs. (She never did let me in.) From France onward, however, I settled down into a more measured routine. I was able to plan five or six flights ahead, and I felt much more comfortable with this. At each destination, I had enough time (at least two or three days) to contact and meet with local diabetes associations, and to arrange interviews with newspapers, radio and television stations. I had enough time to relax and explore at some locations. It became a balanced combination of busy planning, fascinating meetings, relaxing, and exhilarating flying. It was definitely a dream come true.

The Mission

Originally, I had planned to return to work by July 2003. However, in many ways the successful completion of DWF was just the beginning of spreading positive messages about what you *can* do with diabetes. I decided to spend another year involved with diabetes awareness and fundraising activities, giving talks to Rotary Clubs in the U.S., U.K., Thailand and to the Children With Diabetes annual conference, IDF Congress in Paris, diabetes associations in the U.K. and Ireland, plus aviation groups in the U.S. By mid 2004, the total funds raised for diabetes research from various groups, companies, family and friends stood at $26,000, subsequently distributed to Diabetes U.K. Research Fund, Children With Diabetes Foundation and the ADA Research Foundation. I am very grateful for everyone's generous support.

In November 2004 I felt honored to give a talk to the 10th Anniversary conference of Taking Control of Your Diabetes. TCOYD is a not-for-profit organization founded in 1995 by Dr. Steve Edelman, who was diagnosed with type 1 diabetes in 1970. The mission of TCOYD is "to educate and motivate people with diabetes, and their loved ones, to take a more active role in their condition, in order to live healthier, happier, and more productive lives." TCOYD has grown into a tremendous organization providing educational and inspirational conferences and a wealth of information on managing type 1 and 2 diabetes through the website www.tcoyd.com and Steve's excellent book *Taking Control of Your Diabetes*.

I was also delighted to visit the Joslin Diabetes Center in Boston in October 2004. Early in the last century, Dr. Elliott Joslin was treating patients with type 1 diabetes prior to insulin being discovered in 1922 by Banting and Best. Over the years the Joslin Diabetes Center has developed into one of the world's leading diabetes treatment and research organizations, with 20 hospital-based affiliated centers and satellites, and an international affiliate in the kingdom of Bahrain.

The Flying

After finishing Diabetes World Flight I continued to do *a lot* of flying—I was still catching up on lost time—with another 285 hours logged by the end of 2003, mainly around the Midwest and across to California. I reveled at low-level flight along the Missouri River valley and lakes from Nebraska into

South Dakota. I discovered that if you fly in "ground effect" (low enough height for lift-induced drag to reduce—35 feet or lower for the Baron) over water, there is a disturbance on the surface. When you pull up and look back, it's as if a vacuum pump has flown over the surface for miles behind—exhilarating stuff!

I set two world speed records from Omaha to Cincinnati and Minneapolis. In November I attempted a transcontinental speed record from San Diego to Kittyhawk in North Carolina. This was an amazing but frustrating day. After early morning fog lifted, the weather was crystal clear all the way from San Diego to North Carolina—2,000 miles—with strong tailwinds of 40 knots. The flight was going tremendously well, with two quick refueling stops, but nine hours into the 11-hour flight and after nightfall, something suddenly started vibrating. I couldn't determine the cause, but I could see the left engine fuel flow needle distinctly flickering. Something had clearly broken. It was better to be safe than sorry. Bitterly disappointed, I landed short in Tennessee with airport emergency services waiting by the runway. When I throttled back for landing, the vibration suddenly increased and continued until I shut the engine down. A counterweight had sheered off the propeller hub, creating an imbalance. I was lucky. I was told that another 10 minutes would have seen the counterweights breaking out of the prop spinner and punching holes in the fuselage, right around the avionics wiring and close to my feet. It was a horribly expensive repair, but it would have been a lot more costly and potentially dangerous had the weights broken free in mid-flight. This incident made me think. Thank God it happened over the mainland U.S. and not halfway across the Pacific Ocean during Diabetes World Flight.

In July 2004 I repeated this record flight attempt from San Diego to Kittyhawk and was delighted to complete it successfully in 12 hours, 9 minutes and 3 seconds. It was a tremendous flying endurance experience, and hopefully another one to help demonstrate what people *can* do with diabetes with a practical system in place to ensure safe (flying) activities.

In July 2003, I enjoyed a visit to the Barabara Davis Center for Childhood Diabetes where I met Dr. Peter Chase and Dr. Bill Jackson. Peter Chase has written an excellent "Pink Panther" book called *Understanding Diabetes* that I have enjoyed reading. He also started me on Lantus insulin, for which I am very grateful. It has improved my diabetes control and quality of life. Bill Jackson gave me a rigorous eye examination, explaining the retinal photographs in great detail. I was immensely relieved to find that my eyes are in good shape. In the mid 1990s, I remember being told that 80% of people with type 1 diabetes require eye treatment (due to retinopathy) after 15 years of having diabetes. This statistic may be out of date now, but regardless, it acts as a powerful motivator to strive hard for good control. (If you have diabetes, be sure to get a yearly dilated eye exam. Retinopathy is treatable with painless laser surgery, and when it is discovered early and treated, you can save your eyesight for a lifetime.)

One thing that I have found since changing to using Lantus insulin with rapid-acting insulin, is that my blood sugar control when flying is much more stable and predictable. I find I can usually keep my sugars between 100–160, ideal for the required flying range and also a good personal range. This is the sort of information that various aviation bodies around the world need to see.

In May 2003 I felt humbled, excited and honored to receive the "Pilot of the Year 2003" award from *Flyer* magazine in the U.K. While several round-the-world flights are made each year, DWF was chosen because of its mission to overcome and try to change blanket discrimination against pilots with medical conditions such as diabetes. I was very grateful to *Flyer* UK for their recognition of DWF and thereby helping to raise more awareness of flying with diabetes.

At the end of 2003, I gave a presentation to the Thai Department of Aviation (DOA) Medical Branch. The DOA had accepted my U.S. license credentials but still did not allow local people with insulin-dependent diabetes to fly. After the presentation, I was delighted to be told that a proposal would be made to adopt the U.S. system for flying with diabetes. It is refreshing to find such a positive attitude. I plan to contact other aviation authorities with details of DWF and the associated in-flight blood sugar control data. Ultimately I hope that more aviation authorities around the world will adopt a similar system for flying safely with diabetes.

One encouraging story I've heard since completing the flight is an excellent example of positive flexibility by the military, and hopefully, one that other military and regulatory bodies can use. It's also a great example of the (Diabetes UK) spirit of equal opportunity based on individual assessment. Staff Sergeant Mark A. Thompson, is deployed with the 1st Infantry Division to Tikrit, Iraq. He developed type 1 diabetes five years ago at the age of 23 and immediately started learning all he could about diabetes and how to control it. He controlled it well enough to continue being in the Army, but to go to Iraq, he had to prove to his commanders and a medical review officer that he could take care of his diabetes in the desert heat and under the unpredictable demands of being in a war zone. He found an insulated pouch to keep the insulin cool (below 85°F), but the 50 pounds of gear he had to wear was more of a challenge. The weight of the body armor broke the first insulin pump. Fortunately he had developed two worst-case scenario plans, which included bringing a spare pump and enough syringes and insulin to last weeks until a replacement could be shipped to him.

Sgt. Thompson is a career counselor and made a strong case to his commanders for allowing him to go to Iraq. He didn't feel that he could recruit new soldiers if he had never been in a combat zone himself. He is proactive with his diabetes and asks for no special provisions. He says, "It's not as important what type of disease a person has, but what type of person has the disease." While he's helping create the new version of what a person with diabetes can do, he's also setting a great example for everyone to follow.

What I Learned about Diabetes

From Diabetes World Flight, I learned many things. Diabetes is a worldwide epidemic. We need to spread public awareness of diabetes, somehow reduce the numbers of people getting it by educating everyone about how to *prevent* it, and educate those who already have it about how to control it well, which is the way to turn off needless discrimination against people with diabetes in every country. We desperately need to improve accessibility and affordability of treatment in third world countries. We need to raise funds for diabetes research to continue improving the tools we use for diabetes management and to find a cure.

Although diabetes appears in every country, at least for type 2 diabetes, it can be prevented or postponed if people will make lifestyle changes. Prevention is one key to saving the people and the healthcare systems that they depend on. The lifestyle changes, which are needed in every country I visited including the United States, can prevent diabetes for those who don't already have it—and lead to good control for those who do. The approach is the same: Healthy food choices and daily exercise, such as walking. We need to change society, and we're all in this together. Taking responsibility for our own lives is key to making the changes stick.

On a personal basis, I would say to anyone with, or without diabetes, if you have a dream—*go for it!* Diabetes cannot stop you from putting your mind to anything and doing it. The past three years of Diabetes World Flight have undoubtedly been the most fulfilling of my life. If the same military doctor had to confirm my diabetes diagnosis now, thanks to the U.S. FAA system for flying, he would have to say something different: "You are a diabetic, and you are *still* a pilot."

> *Youth is not a time of life; it is a state of mind…Nobody grows old merely by a number of years. We grow old by deserting our ideals. Years may wrinkle the skin, but to give up enthusiasm wrinkles the soul.*
>
> —Samuel Ullman, 1840–1924

Resources

American Association of Diabetes Educators
1-800-Team-UP-4
www.aadenet.org

American Diabetes Association (ADA)
1-800-DIABETES (342-2383)
www.diabetes.org

Barbara Davis Center for Childhood Diabetes in Denver
www.barbaradaviscenter.org

Children With Diabetes
www.childrenwithdiabetes.org

Diabetes U.K.
www.diabetes.org.uk

Diabetes World Flight
www.diabetesworldflight.com

International Diabetes Federation (IDF)
www.idf.org

Joslin Diabetes Centers
617-732-2400
www.joslin.org

Richard Bernstein: www.diabetes-normalsugars.com

Ron Raab: www.diabetes-low-carb.org

Taking Control of Your Diabetes: www.tcoyd.com

Books
Agatston, Arthur, MD. *The South Beach Diet*
Atkins, Robert C., MD. *Dr. Atkins' New Diet Revolution*
Bernstein, Richard K., MD. *Dr. Bernstein's Diabetes Solution*
Edelman, Steve, MD. *Taking Control of Your Diabetes*
English, Dave. *Slipping the Surly Bonds: Great Quotations on Flight*
Gann, Ernest. *Fate is the Hunter*
Loy, Spike and Bo. *Getting a Grip on Diabetes.*
Polonsky, William, PhD. *Diabetes Burnout*
Porter, Lance. *28 Days to Diabetes Control!*
Tair, Cliff. *Flight of the Kiwi*

Appendix 1 – Medical requirements for flying with insulin-dependent diabetes in the USA

Once a normal Class III Medical exam has been done, all diabetes-related reports must be sent to the FAA medical appeals branch. Reports need to include the following information:

- The applicant must be receiving insulin treatment for at least six months prior to application
- No recurrent hypoglycemic reactions resulting in the loss of consciousness, seizure, impaired cognitive function or requiring intervention by another person within the past 5 years
- No evidence of hypoglycemic unawareness within the past 5 years. If a hypoglycemic attack has been experienced, there must be one year of demonstrated stability following the first episode. If such events can be explained, however, the FAA may still award you the medical to fly
- Any accident or incidents involving motor vehicles, regardless of the reason
- An endocrinologist's evaluation, including A1C levels, insulin dosage, diet, any peripheral neuropathy, circulatory deficiency or other diabetes-related complication
- An ophthalmologist's report confirming the absence of any clinically significant eye disease, especially retinopathy
- Verification by a doctor of the applicant's understanding of diabetes and ability to control and manage blood glucose levels

Once the Third Class medical is issued, it is valid for one year only. Every three months, your doctor's report must include the following:

- Evaluation of A1C and overall control
- Evaluation of daily blood sugar test results. (With monitors' memory banks and PC download facility, this requirement can now be met more easily.) These results must be available to the FAA if requested
- Information on any loss of control or hypoglycemic event, and any accidents involving motor vehicles
- In the fourth report, the findings of the annual exams done by the endocrinologist and ophthalmologist must also be sent to the FAA.

Finally, at 5-year intervals, you will need a stress ECG test.

Index